# INSIGHT COMPACT GUIDES

# MaDeira

*Compact Guide: Madeira* is the ultimate quick-reference guide to this classic destination. It tells you all you need to know about Madeira's attractions, from dramatic cliffs to peaceful fishing villages, lush valleys to exotic gardens and stunning vistas to vintage wines.

This is just one title in *Apa Publications'* new series of pocket-sized, easy-to-use guidebooks intended for the independent-minded traveller. *Compact Guides* pride themselves on being up-to-date and authoritative. They are in essence miniature travel encyclopedias, designed to be comprehensive yet portable, as well as readable and reliable.

*Janet Showat*

## Star Attractions

An instant reference to some of Madeira's most interesting attractions to help you on your way.

*Funchal p20*

*Fortress of São Lourenço p26*

*Museum of Ecclesiastical Art p32*

*Orchid Garden p34*

*Monte p37*

*Machico p39*

*Ponta de São Lourenço p48*

*Pico do Arieiro p53*

*Câmara de Lobos p61*

*Levadas p62*

# Madeira

## Introduction

## Places

## Culture

## Leisure

## Practical Information

# Madeira – Pearl of the Atlantic

*Opposite: view towards
Ponta de São Lourenço*

Those approaching the island of Madeira by air usually see nothing but clouds at first – the mountains and the north coast are often concealed from view. But soon Madeira's deep ravines and steep mountain slopes create a bizarre and stunning landscape. Beneath the sharp volcanic peaks, black, craggy cliffs with tiny emerald-green terraces can be seen rising steeply from the waters of the Atlantic.

*In the Curral Valley*

The land in the south of the island is intensively cultivated, in sharp contrast to the impenetrable jungle in the north and the desolate mountain landscape in the middle. The island's climate is pleasantly moderate all year round: winters are never really cold and, thanks to the proximity of the sea, the summers are never unbearably hot. Madeira's subtropical climate and fertile soil provide ideal conditions for growing almost any plant species on earth, and it is justly famed for its magnificent, colourful blossom – best enjoyed in the spring when its scent mingles with the sharp tang of the sea breezes. But Madeira has far more to offer: ornate churches, stately mansions and magnificent parks; scenic and exhilarating hiking trails; and above all, fine wines and a unique cuisine appreciated by connoisseurs for centuries. In addition, Madeira is steeped in history enhanced by romantic legends about its discovery, controversy over its historical relations with Portugal and an intriguing British connection. A large proportion of island life is centred around its capital, Funchal. Villages are dotted along the steep coastline and scattered in the mountains, where the appalling poverty can't be ignored. The gulf between the rich and poor on this tiny island is enormous.

**5**

*Scaling fish for a living*

The sparsely populated, neighbouring island of Porto Santo, with its splendid golden-yellow sandy beaches, is quite different. There's far less greenery, but that's more than compensated for by the wild, desert-like countryside and relaxed atmosphere.

*Funchal in bloom*

Madeira is a place that shouldn't be rushed but slowly sipped and savoured, like its famous fortified wines. The pace of life is sedate. With its warm climate, fantastic scenery, exotic greenery, rich cultural heritage and friendly people, Madeira offers visitors a restful retreat from the hectic pace of 20th-century living.

## Position and size

The Madeira Islands are a volcanic archipelago in the North Atlantic Ocean. They belong to Portugal and comprise of two inhabited islands, Madeira and Porto Santo, and two uninhabited groups, the Desertas and the Selvagens. Madeira itself, the main island, is by far the largest (surface area 741sq km/286sq miles). Porto Santo, the second-largest island, covers just 45sq km (17sq miles). The three uninhabited islands to the southeast of Madeira, known as the Desertas, have a combined surface area of just 1.4sq km (0.5sq miles). The Selvagens, or Salvage Islands, are three rocks 251km (156 miles) south of Madeira towards the Canary Islands, the largest of which has a circumference of about 5km (3 miles). The archipelago's total population of 300,000 lives mostly on the main island. Porto Santo has roughly 5,000 inhabitants.

Madeira lies approximately on the same latitude as the Moroccan town of Casablanca (33°N). The islands are 980km (609 miles) from Lisbon, but only around 600km (373 miles) away from Cap Juby on the African coast southeast of the Canary Island of Fuerteventura. Geographically, the Madeira Islands belong to Africa; politically, to Europe.

**6**

*Seaside pursuits*

## When to go

Any time of year is a good time to visit Madeira, although people planning to swim in the sea should avoid the winter. Winter is an ideal time for hiking trips in the mountains, but remember that temperatures up there can get rather cool. The early springtime is also changeable, but the sheer profusion of blossom more than makes up for that. Summer and autumn are the best times to go to get good weather.

## Climate

Madeira's year-round spring-like climate is legendary. January to March is the coolest time, although even then the temperature rarely falls below 14°C (57°F) at night, with daytime temperatures often reaching 18°C (64°F) or more. The sea is quite cold for swimming during wintertime (17°C/62°F). The moderate influence of the Atlantic means that temperatures hardly ever exceed 25°C (77°F) during the summer months, and the evenings stay mild and pleasant. The south coasts of Madeira and Porto Santo are the only places where the temperature remains warm throughout the year; the cloudy northern part of Madeira is often several degrees cooler. The higher the altitude, the greater the differences in winter, summer, day and night temperatures. It's actually very rare for summer temperatures on Madeira to exceed 30°C (86°F), but they do whenever the *Leste*, a hot African wind, blows from the southeast. If the *Leste* blows in winter it promises several days of fine weather – ideal for trips into the mountains.

It rarely rains on Madeira or Porto Santo between June and September, but the weather during the rest of the year can be changeable.

## Nature and the environment

The highest mountain on Madeira is the Pico Ruivo (1,862m/6,108ft); several other peaks are only slightly lower. In contrast to the main island, marked by deep ravines and steep cliffs, Porto Santo is fairly flat: its Pico de Facho reaches only 517m (1,696ft). Both islands are of volcanic origin, despite their differing appearance: they are the summits of gigantic mountains that have their bases on a seemingly bottomless ocean floor at roughly 4,000m (13,120ft) below sea level.

No volcanic activity has been recorded since the islands were discovered in 1351, although small eruptions are thought to have taken place around 1,000 years ago. Madeira has only a few small, dark, and very pebbly beaches, where swimming isn't much fun; artificial pools have therefore been created in the rocks, allowing swimming in sea water as well as in lava pools. Porto Santo, however, has an 8-km (5-mile) long, golden sandy beach considered one of the best in the Atlantic.

**Flora:** Madeira's famous blossom has earned it the nickname 'The Floating Garden', and is certainly one of the main reasons why so many people come. Most visitors to the island stay in the south, with its pleasant climate and its parks and gardens brimming over with the different coloured blossoms of all kinds of tropical and subtropical plants. The beautiful blooms aren't just a privilege of the rich either: rows of magnificent ornamental plants can be seen outside the smallest hut, often growing out of old plastic buckets or oil drums. Few people today realise that all this blossom only arrived on the islands during the 18th century, when the English wine merchants moved to Madeira bringing plants from all over the world for their gardens. The inhabitants of the small English colony here used to hold regular competitions to see who possessed the latest botanical rarity.

During the winter, the most noticeable plants are the enormous poinsettia bushes; the camellias also begin to bloom at the beginning of the year in Blandy's Garden and elsewhere. At the end of April, the avenues of Funchal turn a gentle purple colour when the rosewood blossom appears (even before the leaves do). Riverbeds and walls are overgrown with violet bougainvillea, and African flame trees produce their dark red flowers. Unlike most Mediterranean countries, Madeira has no dry season in summer, so blossom continues to grow in profusion. In the autumn the enormous silk-cotton trees produce their beautiful violet flowers, and their seedcases, which resemble cotton, can be seen flying through the streets in spring.

Madeira's mountainous interior presents a different picture entirely. The forests of eucalyptus are filled with belladonna lilies in the autumn, and in springtime pale yellow

*Madeira is famous for its blossom*

7

*Hibiscus*

*Haven for black swans at Monte*

*Giant ferns*

acacia can be seen covering large areas of the south-facing slopes. The north of the island contains vast expanses of laurel forest, forming a green jungle with innumerable species of tree and shrub, as well as enormous daisies, geraniums and foxgloves that can't be found anywhere else in the world. Dripping wet lichen hangs from the trees, and there are all kinds of different ferns and mosses. Even in this humid region, man has been active: the gardens are full of attractive rhododendrons, azaleas and agapanthus (African lily) with their large blue and white blooms, and in summer the village streets are lined with magnificent hydrangeas. High in the mountains, the gnarled forests of briar are covered with beautiful white flowers in the springtime. Up here, winter nights are always freezing but daytime temperatures can get quite warm, creating extreme conditions so that the flora generally resembles that of the Alps. A rarity that takes quite a bit of finding, by the way, is the famous yellow Madeira violet.

**Fauna:** Travellers to Madeira are often amazed at how little visible wildlife there seems to be on the island. Of course it's far harder for animals to make the journey across the Atlantic than to plant seeds and spores, and the bats, birds and insects arrived accidentally, all by themselves. Therefore it's not surprising that birds (roughly 200 species) and insects (around 700 species) make up the largest groups, but they are still a rare sight. Many species of bird have been reduced in number by hunters; some, such as the Madeiran ring-dove, have been brought to the verge of extinction. Birds of prey such as buzzards and falcons have had better chances of survival, as have smaller species such as the commonly sighted Madeiran kinglet or the Madeiran chaffinch.

As far as insects are concerned, many of the varieties on Madeira have lost the ability to fly, and so are hard to spot. Others have fallen victim to insecticides used in agriculture. Mosquitoes are, thankfully, rare. There are no snakes, but several species of frog, whose spawn may have reached the island inside the feathers of seabirds.

The sea around Madeira isn't all that rich in fish, mainly because there is no continental shelf. Overfishing and the technique of dynamite fishing – which is now illegal – have also contributed to the scarcity of aquatic life. The most commonly caught fish is the *espada,* or cutlass fish (*see page 81*), which is brought up from the depths with the aid of long rods and of which there seems to be an unlimited supply. The same cannot be said of the tuna fish, whose numbers have dwindled considerably since the late 1980s. Several steps have now been taken to preserve aquatic life off the coast: the area around the islands has been declared a nature reserve, and several species, notably mammals, have been placed under protection and are now gradually multiplying once more. This applies in particular to the sperm whale and the Mediterranean monk seal. There are only 12 of these seals left in a colony living on the uninhabited Desertas.

*Cod drying at Machico*

*At the fish market in Funchal*

9

**Levadas:** The narrow canals all over Madeira used for transporting water for irrigation purposes are known as *levadas*. Many Mediterranean countries have had similar irrigation systems since Roman times, but nowhere have they been brought to such a peak of perfection. The network of canals and their tributaries on Madeira is around 5,000km (3,100 miles) long; the main canals alone have a combined length of 1,500km (930 miles). Legend has it that Moorish slaves gave Madeira its first *levadas*, and it has been proven that sugar cane plantations on the islands had their own irrigation systems as early as the 15th century. At that time there were many freshwater springs in the southern part of Madeira, and so the first *levadas* were probably only a few hundred metres long. When the island switched over to viniculture during the mid-16th century the systems fell into disuse, because wine did not need irrigating. It was only with the reintroduction of sugar cane cultivation in the 19th century that the *levadas* were resurrected. In the meantime the island had become a lot drier, and the water then had to be brought from springs and waterfalls in the rainier northern region. The curving *levadas* were created across stretches of several miles, sloping slightly all the way. This stupendous engineering achievement was gruelling work for the builders, who only had pickaxes with which to hack the channels out of the stone.

Water consumption has increased steadily since then, and the *levada* network is still being extended – most recently thanks to funds from the European Union. Nowadays, the water doesn't follow gravity but travels through

*Toboggan driver in Monte*

*Lazy days in Machico*

*Fun and games in Funchal*

pipes and tunnels and across bridges to prevent contamination and evaporation, irrigating the land for the island's staple banana crops. But the old *levadas* are still essential to Madeira; they're also ideal for hikers, who can comfortably follow their courses through the steepest ravines without having to deal with any steep gradients. Madeira has *levadas* to suit everyone's taste: some are broad and easy-going, and lined with bushes in bloom; others are incredibly narrow, affording dizzying glimpses into seemingly bottomless ravines far below.

## Population

Visitors from Europe may be surprised at how conservative and conventional the Madeirans seem to be. The men and women appear to live in entirely separate worlds. The men – middle-class and often the only wage earners in the family – meet up in pubs and bars after work to play cards, or at weekends to play football. For the women, washing machines and refrigerators are still a sign of social prestige; working-class wives meet up regularly at the local wash centres. The women continue to look after all issues regarding the household and child-rearing; extended families are common, with all members selflessly looking after each other's interests and forming an effective substitute for the Portuguese welfare system (which still leaves much to be desired). There is little room for individuality, and few people dare to break with the majority for fear of becoming social outcasts. Customs are changing fast among the young, however, and the traditional division of roles between the sexes is becoming less clear cut.

Madeira is quite densely populated (350 inhabitants per sq km). On the south coast, especially around Funchal, it is rare to find any land that is not built-up. The little terraced fields are packed tightly together, with the poverty-stricken homes of the rural population crammed in between. Along the coast road, it is hard to tell when one parish runs into another. The villages usually comprise a few bars, shops and houses huddled around a church, as the farmers live close to their fields. Indeed, around 90 percent of the population of Madeira is jammed into the narrow coastal strip in the south of the island. Hardly any houses are built above the cloud level of 500m (1,640ft). The north of the island is far less populated; there's hardly any room for agriculture here either, since the slopes often fall steeply down to the sea. The north's rainy climate is also too harsh for such sensitive crops as bananas or sugar cane. As for Madeira's mountainous interior, where nature can be experienced in its purest form, it is almost completely uninhabited.

**Ethnic background:** The Portuguese discovered the uninhabited Madeiran archipelago at the beginning of the 15th century and divided up the land between themselves, their friends and their relatives. Slaves were brought across from North Africa and the Canary Islands and labourers were hired from Portugal. At that time slaves made up as much as ten percent of the population. Soon a new system of land management, the *colonia*, was introduced: a landlord lived in Funchal and spent only part of the year on his estates, which he parcelled up into tiny areas often measuring less than an acre. Leaseholders known as *colonos* were recruited to look after them. In this way, many people without land of their own came to Madeira, especially from northern Portugal. The *colonos* had to provide the landlords with one half of their annual produce allowing them to live well in the city while their impoverished tenants continued to slave away in the fields. This leaseholder system was only finally abolished after Portugal's revolution of 1974. Since that time, many *colonos* have been able to buy their land with the help of cheap state loans, although even today the areas of land in question are just as small as ever.

The population of Madeira today is predominantly of northern Portuguese extraction. Moorish, Black-African and Canary-Island slaves also played a significant role, although many returned to their home countries after slavery was abolished.

Outsiders have played an important role in the economic development of Madeira. Around the year 1500 numerous merchants active in the sugar business settled in Funchal: they came from Italian city-states (the most famous of these was Christopher Columbus, who lived as a sugar trader on Madeira for several years before his voyage to the New World), and also from Flanders, which at that time had close relations with Portugal. Later on it was the English who exerted the most profound influence on Madeira.

Portugal had been under Spanish rule from 1580 to 1640 and had finally regained its independence thanks to British help. The English promptly secured the monopoly in the Portuguese wine trade. At the end of the 17th century and especially in the early part of the 18th century, numerous English wine merchants came to Madeira to ship wine home to England and to its colonies. Later they became active in the cultivation and production of wine and played a considerable role in producing what is today known as Madeira wine. The 300 or so British families who lived on Madeira kept themselves very much to themselves, and formed a community that soon dominated the islands' political and economic life. The crisis in the wine trade at the end of the 19th century forced several of them to turn their backs on Madeira, although even today there are still several influential English families living on the islands.

11

*Christopher Columbus*

*Shipping home the wine*

To many of Madeira's early inhabitants, the archipelago was little more than an easy stopover on the way to Brazil. When the wine trade entered its recession at the end of the 19th century, many people on Madeira were faced with financial ruin. Emigration increased dramatically and continued unabated right up to the 1970s. Favourite destinations were Venezuela and South Africa, which has an estimated Madeiran population today of around 100,000. After the Portuguese revolution of 1974, many emigrants returned to Madeira because of the new economic opportunities it promised. They opened restaurants, bars and supermarkets, many of them with exotic-sounding names such as *Luanda* or *Minas Gerais*. There has also been a heavy influx of emigrants returning home from South Africa, although recent developments there may have helped to stem the tide.

*Christ in the Cathedral*

## Religion

The Madeiran population is mostly Roman Catholic, apart from a small Anglican minority. Religion still plays an important role for the rural population, although in Funchal and the larger municipalities elderly women seem to make up the majority of the congregations. The young people tend to be present only at marriages, baptisms and communions, which are still lavishly celebrated.

*Folk ensemble*

## Language

The Portuguese spoken on Madeira has several South American elements – the result of the islands' close contact with Brazil. Emigrants back from Venezuela have Spanish accents. The centuries-long British influence on Madeira is omnipresent, however, and foreigners are regularly addressed in English. Some islanders speak the language almost perfectly, while others only know a few phrases. Most Madeirans will automatically classify visitors to their islands as English (*Ingles*).

## Economy

Bananas are the staple of the Madeiran economy and there are extensive plantations all around Funchal and along the southern coastal strip. The climate in the north of the island is too harsh for their cultivation. The irrigation canals known as *levadas* (*see page 9*) provide the plantations with the precious water they need; and bananas need a great deal, especially during the dry summer months (one kilogram of bananas can require as much as 1,000 litres).

However, Madeira's banana industry has earned itself a bad name over the past few years: high costs and the large amount of manual labour used have almost resulted in its demise. Indeed, the industry would not have survived this long if it had not been for Portugal's decision to impose

a high levy on its other imported bananas. Madeira has thus been Portugal's sole banana supplier for several years – a situation that is no longer tenable now that the markets have been opened up within the European Union. At one stage Madeira's banana industry seemed threatened with extinction, when Portugal seemed on the point of being swamped by cheap Caribbean bananas imported via other EU countries. But Brussels saw reason and the import restrictions introduced in 1993 have been keeping prices in the EU artificially high, giving temporary respite to Madeira. Critics have been warning of the ecological consequences of heavy banana cultivation, but alternative concepts are still in their infancy.

For centuries, wine was almost the only source of income for the island, and vineyards were created wherever climate and soil permitted. One year's grain harvest was not even enough to support the population for three months, and basic foodstuffs have always been imported. A crisis in the wine industry meant famine, and this is what happened in 1852 and 1872, when mildew and phylloxera were accidentally imported from America, causing severe damage to Madeira's wine harvest. Phylloxera-resistant American grapes were duly imported in the hope that they would replace the European ones, but wines derived from these grapes possess a sharp aftertaste, and are generally scorned by connoisseurs. The good reputation Madeira wines had enjoyed for so long was almost ruined beyond repair at one stage, and it's only recently that efforts have been made to restore quality and to compete again with sherry and port. American grapes are still being grown in many areas of the island, producing a light, sweet red wine with a slightly fruity taste. This wine is only available from the barrel, and is extremely popular with the locals – so much so, in fact, that the annual yield is frequently consumed within a few months.

*Bananas or bust*

**13**

*Vintage years*

*Sour grapes*

*Embroidery for sale*

*Tool of the wickerwork trade*

During the last century, feverish attempts were made to find new products that could be exported in order to save the island's economy from impending disaster. Bananas played a certain role even then, but the islanders placed most of their hopes on sugar cane, which had already helped them prosper back in the 15th century. Small cane-processing factories sprang up all over the island, producing sugar and also *Aguardente de Cana*, a kind of rum. Production was too costly, though, and the climate was too cool and dry for sugar cane, which is really a tropical crop. The only export market was that of Portugal, which fended off imports from other countries by imposing high duties. The sugar cane industry thus gradually dwindled in importance as the 20th century progressed, and today only a few small fields remain next to the two remaining distilleries in Porto da Cruz and Calheta.

When the Madeirans speak of their island's industry, they are usually referring to embroidery, the widespread handicraft organised as a cottage industry by a handful of factories. Embroidery employs around 30,000 people, almost all of them women from poor families who earn a meagre living in this way. It was introduced to Madeira during the first severe recession in the wine trade (in the middle of the last century) by Elisabeth Phelps, the daughter of an English wine merchant. She had blouses, dresses and table napkins embroidered in the English style, which were then sold to London's high society. Around the turn of the century, several German merchants settled on Madeira and developed the embroidery trade into a real industry. In the factory the material to be embroidered is marked with blue dye through a stencil. The actual embroidery is then done at home, but the procedure doesn't end there: back in the factory the material is washed, ironed, sewn, cleaned, folded and packed, and given its

leaden seal of authenticity. The use of machinery is strictly forbidden. Everything is made by hand, and the price is correspondingly high.

The island's wickerwork industry is organised on a similar basis. Many farmers in the rainy northern and northeastern regions of Madeira earn a living by planting willow bushes and selling the osiers to weaving workshops. Most of these are in Camacha, where the craft was first introduced to the island by the English during the 19th century. The factory delivers orders to the wickerworkers, who normally run small family businesses; the goods are then varnished and either sold locally or exported worldwide.

Tourism is the islanders' biggest hope for the future. It began during the 19th century when wealthy Europeans came to spend winter in Madeira, hoping to cure all kinds of maladies ranging from tuberculosis to gout. For many years Madeira was an exclusive travel destination for the very rich, with just a handful of luxury hotels, notably Reid's Hotel. Mass tourism only really began during the 1980s, and there are still only 20,000 beds on the island. New hotels and holiday villages are being built with the aid of EU funds, which will also be used to restore many old mansions and grand hotels. Originally, tourism on Madeira centred around Funchal, but now the other, smaller communities on the island are growing increasingly popular with visitors. Caniço is being turned into Madeira's second most important tourist centre, with Machico and the neighbouring Porto Santo not far behind.

*On the verandah of Reid's Hotel*

## Politics

The revolution in Portugal in 1974 marked the transition from dictatorship to democracy in that country, which had far-reaching consequences for Madeira and its islands. Formerly entirely dependent on Lisbon for all political decisions, Madeira now hoped for a certain measure of self-determination. The independence movement known as FLAMA wanted to sever all ties with Portugal completely, but failed to have its way. During the first elections in 1975, moderate forces prevailed both on Madeira and in Portugal itself, and one year later the archipelago received the status of an autonomous region (RAM). Important decisions are still made in Lisbon as before, and a so-called Minister of the Republic supervises the island's government and parliament to ensure that their decisions do not conflict too seriously with Portuguese interests. The regional parliament, composed of 50 elected members, has the power to make decisions relating to the regional budget and legislative issues where the islands are concerned. The executive branch of the governing party is made up of the president, vice-president and six secretaries, each with various responsibilities and concerns.

*The Madeiran flag*

# Historical Highlights

**1351** Madeira appears for the first time on a Genoese map known as the Laurentian portolano. It is referred to as *Isola di Logname* ('island of wood'). The Portuguese translate this name later into their language (*madeira* = wood).

**1373** Treaty of friendship signed between England and Portugal after the marriage of Philippa of Lancaster to the Portuguese King John I. They later have a son, Prince Henry the Navigator.

**1418** Henry the Navigator sponsors two of his naval commanders, João Gonçalvez Zarco and Tristão Vaz Teixeira, to explore the African coast. Having been blown off course, they take shelter on an island which they call Porto Santo. Two years later, during a second voyage, they discover the much larger uninhabited island of Madeira. The two commanders are accompanied on this voyage by Bartolomeu Perestrelo, an Italian entrepreneur, who subsequently becomes governor of Porto Santo.

**1440–50** Having established themselves on Madeira, Zarco and Tristão Vaz are given half shares in the island and divide it up between their friends and relatives, many of whom begin cultivating sugar.

**1452** The first consignment of slaves – negroes from Africa and Guanches from the Canaries – is shipped over to Madeira to work in the lucrative sugar-cane plantations and begins constructing *levadas*, the island's vast network of irrigation channels. Madeira soon becomes Europe's most important supplier of sugar. Wine and grain are also produced.

**1478** Christopher Columbus sails into Funchal harbour on a trading mission to buy sugar. That same year he marries the governor of Porto Santo's daughter, Felipa Moniz, and settles on the island for a short period. According to popular belief, the couple subsequently live in Felipa's father's house on Porto Santo where debris washed up on the beaches fuels Coumbus's ambitions of discovering the New World.

**1480 onwards** Various contingents of settlers arrive from Europe. Many of them are merchants who invest in the sugar plantations and the extensive irrigation systems. Maintaining their connections with the world of high finance and the commercial centres of Europe, the newcomers often perform the triple role of landowner-merchant-financier.

**1495** Following the accession of Manuel I to the the throne of Portugal, patronage of the island of Madeira passes to the Portuguese Crown. This puts an end to frequent outbreaks of open resistance to the Crown by the island's noble families.

**1514** Madeira's population reaches 5,000.

**1530 onwards** The importance of the sugar trade begins to decline in the face of fiercer competition from Brazil and Central America. The island's once fertile soil is also exhausted. By the mid-16th century many of the sugar plantations on Madeira have been replaced by vines from Cyprus and Crete.

**1542** Completion of a town wall with ramparts around Funchal, built as a defence against constant attacks by pirates.

**1566** Lured by rumours of the enormous wealth of Funchal, Bertrand de Montluc, a nobleman at the court of King Charles IX, arrives in the bay on October 3 with a squadron of ships. With the regular governor away in Lisbon, the invaders meet little resistance and the new defences prove totally inadequate. Inside the Palace of São Lourenço, some 250 people are put to the sword, including the temporary governor and his family. The French ransack the island for two weeks and the ships' holds are crammed with costly furnishings plundered from the homes of the wealthy, together with silver taken from Madeira's monasteries and convents and the stocks of the big mercantile houses. Thousands of wine casks are split open and left to run dry.

**1569** King Sebastião grants permission for the founding of a Jesuit College.

**1580–1640** The death of the last in line to the Portuguese throne places Portugal under Spanish rule, and Madeira is drawn into the conflict between Spain and England. The Madeiran coast is subjected to repeated raids by English corsairs.

**17th century** A new era commences, with Madeira at the centre of trade routes between Europe, Africa and North and South America. After King Charles II's marriage to Catherine of Braganza in 1662, many British merchants begin to settle in Madeira to take advantage of Charles's protectionist policies on trade. The 1665 ban on the export of European goods to English colonies does not include Madeira, so British merchants can ship wine from Madeira to the American colonies.

**1703** Anglo-Portuguese trade relations are normalised under the terms of the Methuen Treaty. England, which has supported Portugal's struggle for independence from Spain, demands numerous concessions in return. English merchants gain a commanding position in the trade of Portugal. The Madeiran wine trade is placed entirely under English control, and many English wine merchants settle on the island.

**1761** The ban on the purchase of slaves in Africa leads to the abolition of slavery on Madeira. A decree to this effect, issued by the enlightened Duke of Pombal, is published in Funchal in 1775.

**1768** Captain Cook anchors at Madeira on his first voyage in the *Endeavour*.

**1803** The rivers in Funchal burst their banks. Over 600 people are drowned in the floods.

**1761** After Dom Miguel proclaims himself absolute monarch of Portugal, the new governor, José Maria Monteiro, arrives with a force of a thousand troops. Many locally important people either flee to Britain or are arrested and exiled to Portuguese colonies.

**1807–14** In response to the French occupation of mainland Portugal during the Napoleonic Wars, the British station 2,000 soldiers on Madeira. Many of these remain on the island once the war is over.

**1856** Elizabeth Phelps, the daughter of a wine merchant, introduces a commercial aspect to Madeira's traditional art of embroidery.

**Mid-19th century onwards** Tourism begins to grow into one of Madeira's major sources of income. Wealthy English people, writers and politicians, and affluent travellers from other European countries come to discover the island and enjoy a life of luxury in the hotels of Funchal.

**1872** Phylloxera, imported by accident from America, destroys most of the vines on Madeira. The wine industry never really recovers from this blow and a large wave of emigration ensues. Bananas replace the vine as the main cash crop, becoming the most important branch of the island's economy.

**1916** In response to a request by the British, Portugal confiscates all German possessions on Madeira. A German submarine promptly surfaces off the coast and sinks a French warship in Funchal harbour.

**1939–45** World War II results in the temporary closure of Reid's Hotel. Some 2,000 refugees from Gibraltar are accommodated on the island, relieving some of the financial hardship caused by the lack of tourists.

**1931** The so-called 'Hunger Revolt' takes place on Madeira after the landowners gain the monopoly on flour imports. The rebellion is finally quelled by forces sent in from Lisbon.

**1947** The first scheduled air links, using seaplanes, are introduced between England, Portugal and Madeira.

**1960** An airport is opened on Porto Santo; four years later, another one is completed on Madeira.

**1974–5** After Portugal's revolution in 1974, the separatist movement known as FLAMA is formed on Madeira. It intercedes for Madeiran independence from Portugal, but fails in its aims.

**1976** Madeira becomes an 'autonomous region' within Portugal. Tourism begins to play an increasingly important role.

**1986** Portugal becomes a member of the European Community.

**1992** The 500th anniversary of the discovery of America rekindles local interest in Christopher Columbus.

**1993** Creation of the European Union single market, which is expected to result in increasing prosperity for Madeira.

*Flower market in Funchal*

*Preceding pages: Funchal from Monte*

*Waterfront kiosk*

# Route 1

## ★★★ Funchal

Funchal is the capital of Madeira and by far the largest town on the island (pop. 120,000 including the suburbs). Nine out of ten tourists visiting Madeira spend their holidays here. Despite the tourists, life in Funchal continues very much as normal. Its bustling markets, shopping streets and harbour are all full of activity. The special atmosphere of its little street cafés or the beach promenade can be enjoyed during the day, and in the evening people meet up in the elegant restaurants of the hotel quarter or in the cosy pubs in the old part of town.

Funchal has a host of worthwhile sights: dignified town houses with leafy inner courtyards, mansions surrounded by subtropical parks, churches, monasteries and fascinating museums. Its wonderful setting, beneath a backdrop of mountains, adds further to its appeal.

### History

When João Gonçalvez Zarco first landed on Madeira in 1419, he set up base at nearby Câmara de Lobos. Shortly afterwards the forests in Funchal Bay were felled and burned, and the fire is said to have got out of control. It was six years before Zarco transferred his residence to Funchal, from where he ruled over the half of the island officially presented to him in 1440 by the throne of Portugal. In 1497 King Manuel I united the two fiefs, and Funchal was declared the island's capital.

The name Funchal comes from the Portuguese for wild fennel (*funcho*) which grew along the banks of the rivers flowing into the bay, but this soon had to make way for the new sugar-cane plantations. By 1500, sugar exports had transformed Funchal into a flourishing metropolis, attracting merchants from all over Europe. The local nobility also preferred to live in the city, and left the management of their estates in more distant parts of the island to tenant farmers.

One historical event will probably remain indelibly etched on Madeira's collective memory: a two-week raid by some French pirates on Funchal in 1566. They plundered and murdered, burning everything in sight, before departing with their near-priceless booty. The pirate chieftain, Bertrand de Montluc, had actually set his sights on the legendary Gold Coast, but his fleet of eight galleons and crew of around a thousand men needed a break along the way, and Madeira's wealth at that time was almost legendary, with its magnificent palaces full of sugar and wine, jewellery and valuable trinkets, and the churches containing much gold and silver. Montluc landed almost unnoticed on a beach west of Funchal, and the town was taken with hardly any resistance.

Many of the inhabitants had fled to the Fortress of São Lourenço which, although it contained several cannons, unfortunately had no cannonballs or powder. So the pirates successfully stormed the fortress and killed everyone inside. Around 250 people are thought to have died. The intruders then raided the island's churches and palaces, tearing out everything they could and at the same time committing unspeakable atrocities. Miraculously, the cathedral's treasure remained untouched; as a wise precaution it had been wrapped in cloths and placed alongside the body of the cathedral treasurer, who had been interred beneath the chancel several days beforehand.

Madeira's days of peace were well and truly over – until this raid, Funchal had been totally unprotected. Fortifications and a town wall were quickly built, the latter being finally razed in the 19th century when the pirate danger had receded for good.

When the sugar business went into recession from the mid-16th century onwards, the island's wine trade began to flourish. From the end of the 17th century, English merchants began arriving in Funchal and built several magnificent mansions on the outskirts of the old city centre.

Many English traders left the island again when the grapevines were hit by phylloxera during the second half of the 19th century. This heralded the start of tourism on Madeira as, during the winter months, the empty mansions were rented out to wealthy foreigners. Madeira was still an exclusive destination in the early part of the 20th century when, under the Salazar dictatorship in Portugal, touristic development was limited to a handful of luxury hotels in Funchal. It wasn't until the 1970s that tourism really began to take off.

**21**

*São Lourenço insignia*

*A wonderful setting*

## Sights

We begin our tour of Funchal at the **Cais Molhe da Pontinha ❶** the great harbour arm with its quay where ferry passengers used to dock in the old days. The Cais and the adjoining section of the beach promenade are the most popular places for a stroll in Funchal; it's here that the locals – and especially the younger people – tend to meet up in the evenings, observing the time-honoured precept of 'to see and be seen'. The rather unseaworthy-looking sailing ship beyond Funchal's small pebbly beach has coloured lights at night, and used to belong to The Beatles. Its present owner had it converted into a restaurant, and it now seems to have found its final mooring.

From the end of the wharf there's a good view of the whole semicircular Bay of Funchal, which is often compared to a seashell; the houses on the slopes extend right up to the cloud line. A century ago the ships in Funchal's **harbour ❷** had to anchor behind a small mole and their passengers and cargoes were then rowed ashore. Today's Cais Molhe da Pontinha only came into being a few

**22**

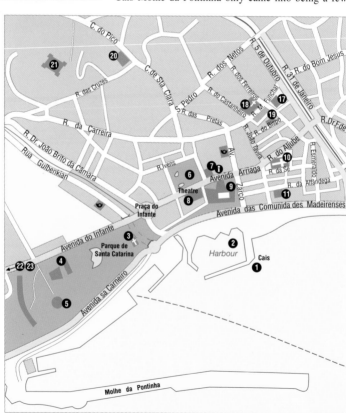

decades ago, and seems rather oversized: Funchal's former importance as a port-of-call on the way to America and Asia has faded in recent years. The ships that bring provisions and depart laden with bananas all moor here, along with several fishing vessels and the ferry that connects with the neighbouring island of Porto Santo. Sometimes the odd cruise ship stops here, too. The most popular time for cruises to visit is around Christmas and New Year, when Funchal's famous firework display takes place; at times the quay is almost too small too accommodate the big ocean liners.

The real jewel of the harbour is the yacht basin, where the transatlantic yachtsmen assemble in autumn just before 'crossing the pond'. They have immortalised themselves in the colourful pictures along the harbour wall. The pictures tend to weather after just a few years, and other yacht crews paint new motifs over them. The fish restaurants down by the marina are exceptionally good, by the way, although the methods they use to attract customers may seem rather pushy.

*Maritime motif at the harbour*

## Funchal Sights 23

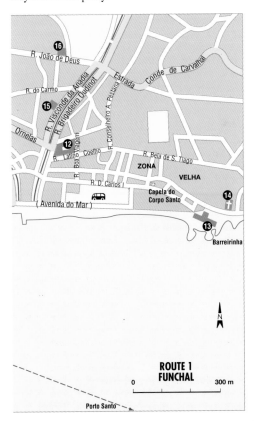

**ROUTE 1 FUNCHAL**

0     300 m

Porto Santo

*The modern shopping centre*

A stroll above the harbour is a good idea at this stage, before continuing to the city centre. On the opposite side of the road is the palace-like facade of the Fortress of São Lourenço (*see page 26*), with Funchal's **theatre** on its left. The rather ugly and incongruous-looking concrete structure next door to these two attractive buildings, which rather destroys the harmony of the traditional architecture, is the modern Marina Shopping Centre.

*St Catherine's Chapel*

Situated on a rise above the harbour, a white **chapel ❸** with steps leading up to it can be seen from afar. It is consecrated to St Catherine, and according to legend stands on the spot where Constança de Almeida, the wife of one of Madeira's discoverers João Gonçalvez Zarco, erected the city's first chapel after Madeira had been claimed by Portugal; no buildings in the city have survived from that time, however. The present chapel dates from the baroque period, and only the font next to the entrance is older; its flower patterns, typical of the local Manueline style – named after the Portuguese king Manuel I – date it to around 1500. It is worth having a close look at the font.

Right next to the chapel is Christopher Columbus (or *Cristovão Colombo* as he is known to the Portuguese), cast in bronze and seemingly enjoying the view out across the harbour. It is said that Columbus spent some time on Madeira from 1479, when he sailed into Funchal harbour on a trading mission to buy sugar. That same year he married the governor of Porto Santo's daughter, Felipa Moniz, and settled in Funchal for a short period.

The adjoining **Santa Catarina Park** is quite breathtaking, with its profusion of blossom, exotic trees, aviaries, a nostalgic café, and the **seaman's monument** in the middle of a vast expanse of lawn. The many park benches here are popular with tourists during the daytime. In the

*Bougainvillaea in Santa Catarina Park*

evening, this is also a favourite spot for courting couples (evenings on Madeira never get really cold all year round). Living conditions on the island are cramped, and most families are still very conservative; they only rarely allow their younger members to meet at home.

In the upper section of the park, directly behind a model windmill that is illuminated at night, a pink-coloured building can be seen shimmering between the trees: the **Quinta Vigia** ❹. A good initial impression of this 18th-century mansion can be obtained by peering through the battle-mented iron gate at the top of the flight of steps. Access today is from the street, via a side door. Don't be deterred by the gentlemen in livery standing guard here; they normally allow curious passers-by to enter (assuming the Quinta Vigia isn't being used for some formal reception by the island's government, that is).

The old house also contains several government offices, and its magnificent grounds can be visited during business hours on weekdays. Painted pink – the traditional colour of mansions on Madeira – the Quinta Vigia was formerly owned by a very wealthy family, hence the small private chapel. The magnificent *azulejos* tiling adorning the first-floor veranda can only be admired from afar, so the best thing to do is to go straight through to the rear section of the gardens, where a small temple-like building can be seen. This is where the women of the house used to sip their afternoon tea while gazing down at the harbour.

25

The Quinta Vigia is often associated with the Empress Elisabeth (Sissi) of Austria: she spent the winter of 1860 on Madeira to recover from a bout of tuberculosis, and also to escape from a marriage crisis with her husband, the Emperor Franz Joseph. But imagining her sitting here sipping tea is, alas, wishful thinking. Despite the fact that several crowned heads have indeed stayed in this house (the Empress Amelia of Brazil, for instance, and her daughter), Sissi never actually spent any time here. For today's Quinta Vigia was once known as Quinta Lambert, which is the only villa left out of five that once overlooked the harbour. The other villas, including the original Quinta Vigia, had to make way for the **casino** ❺ which together with the adjoining Casino Park Hotel forms a rather haphazard-looking mass of concrete.

*Niemeyer's casino*

The Brazilian architect Oscar Niemeyer built the casino in the shape of a crown of thorns, similar to his famous cathedral in Brazil's capital. The destruction of the old *quintas* at the beginning of the 1970s caused much controversy; many local inhabitants were shocked at the alien architectural style. Nevertheless, it's hard to imagine the city skyline without the building today – some people even find it quite attractive in comparison to some of the more recent architectural aberrations.

*Henry the Navigator*

Heading on towards the city centre now, the **Prince's Square** (*Praça do Infante*) comes into view, with fountains surrounding the globe at its centre. A bronze statue of **Prince Henry the Navigator** can be seen at the edge of the square; he is of course famous for only having set sail once in his entire life, but he did sponsor the Portuguese voyages of discovery – and their first success was the acquisition of Madeira in 1419. The statue silhouetted against the square is popular with photographers.

There is a magnificent avenue of rosewood trees here. At the end of April, even before their tender green leaves start to bud, they are covered with a bluish-violet blossom. And not far away, over to the left, is another pretty park, the **Jardim Municipal** ❻. A Franciscan monastery once stood here but its ruins were removed at the end of the last century to make way for the park. The locals relax on the benches here in the shade, reading their newspapers or just watching the world go by. The park is full of tropical plants: palm fern, magnolia, enormous red sandalwood trees with their red blossom, Mexican screw trees, majestic araucarias and silk-cotton trees, to name just a few.

*Sampling some Madeira wine*

Next to the park is the beautiful ★★ **Madeira Wine Company Lodge** ❼, where visitors can not only taste and buy wines but also join the hour-long tour through the premises (Monday to Friday 10.30am and 3.30pm; Saturday 11am). The company was formed by a merger of vintners in the early 20th century, and is today responsible for half of the island's wine exports.

Opposite the Jardim Municipal is the **Chamber of Commerce** ❽. The building housed the Café Ritz until the turn of the century, and the stucco and tiles date from that time. The tiles depict several idyllic scenes from the island's past: wealthy people lying in hammocks, being carried up to the mountain peaks; the old funicular railway to Monte, from where the journey down into the valley continued by gravity-powered toboggan (*Carros de Cesto*); ships anchored in the harbour; wicker basket-makers and women embroiderers; and a dignified-looking ox cart (*Carros de Bois*), once an important means of transport in Funchal until it finally made way for city traffic at the end of the 1970s.

*Fortress of São Lourenço*

Next door the massive walls with hardly any windows belong to the **Fortress of São Lourenço** ❾. A statue of St Lawrence can be seen above the main entrance (the ship that brought João Gonçalvez Zarco to Madeira was also named after the saint). The fortress is still being used for military purposes even today, but one section of it contains several items documenting its history and is open to the public. Just down the street from the fortress, past the green guardhouses, there's a good view of the southeastern tower; built in 1513 during the reign of King Manuel I,

*The Cathedral*

**27**

*Zarco*

it is the oldest part of the building. The Fortress of São Lourenço never actually fulfilled its original function: the outer walls were only completed in the 17th century, by which time the edifice was already outmoded from the military point of view. The interior was then converted into the governor's residence.

Funchal's city centre proper begins at the **monument to João Gonçalvez Zarco**. The side streets here contain rows of souvenir shops selling embroidered products.

Funchal's ★ **Cathedral** (*Sé*) **10** is one of the few buildings in the Manueline style still remaining in the city. It was completed in 1514, having been commissioned 21 years earlier by King Manuel I. The facade is unpretentious, and broken up only by the majestic portal with its elaborate stonework, and by the magnificent rose window above. The gable is crowned by the symbol of the Knights of the Order of the Cross. Before entering the cathedral it's worth taking a look at the apse with its small, elaborate towers and embellished parapet. The square tower has a pointed roof covered with geometrically laid out *azulejo* tiles, which sparkle colourfully in the sunshine.

In the dark interior, several valuable items still survive from the days of the cathedral's foundation: the wooden ceiling, for instance, carved in wood in the Mudejar style, is still in good condition. It was carved from Madeira cedar, which is particularly resistant to woodworm. There is some fine ivory intarsia work, although the details are often hard to make out because of the poor lighting conditions. The carving can best be admired from the small wooden bench up in the right transept, where there is more light. The choir stalls, painted blue and with gilt decoration, also date from the 16th century; they were carved in Flanders and then imported. The altars with their magnificent woodcarving and gold leaf decoration were only added during the baroque period.

*Cathedral interior*

Leave the cathedral now via the small passageway to the left of the altar, admiring the two enormous baroque *azulejos* tiled pictures on the way. The blue-and-white picture to the left depicts a scene from Bethlehem, and on the right is the archangel Michael.

An interesting detour at this point is provided by a walk along the ★ **Rua João Tavira**, just to the left of the cathedral. This street was converted into a pedestrian precinct only recently and given an imaginative black-and-white pavement; the date 1419 is a reminder of the year in which Madeira was claimed by Portugal. During that time twin-masted caravels like the ones depicted here were quite common and often used by the Portuguese on their voyages of discovery. A few steps further on, the points of the compass can be seen, followed by pictures of an ox cart pulling a barrel of wine, a porter wearing typical Madeiran folk dress (leather boots, baggy trousers and a *carapuça*, the traditional small hat with a bobble) and carrying two chickens on a stick across his shoulder, and hammock-bearers carrying a sick man across rough terrain.

*Autonomy Monument*

*The bustling market*

Back at the cathedral turn right towards the harbour where the pedestrian precinct is lined with cafés. On the left shortly before the road beside the harbour is the **Old Customs House** (*Velha Alfândega*) ⑪. The small portal in the Rua da Alfândega with its masonry embellishments and the Portuguese coat of arms above its entrance dates from the original Manueline structure, built on this site in around 1500. The remainder of the building was destroyed during the severe earthquake of 1748, and later completely rebuilt in the baroque style. Today the Old Customs House is the headquarters of the Regional Parliament of Madeira (closed to public access). The modern extension, housing the main conference hall on the side of the building facing the sea, jars somewhat with the rest of the building.

Carry on eastwards now along the street next to the harbour. The **Autonomy Monument** (*Monumento a Autonomia*) can be seen in the middle of a modern-looking square. The rather oddly-shaped column on the landward side of the square is a copy of Funchal's former pillory (*pelourinho*) that stood on this site until 1835. Directly opposite, on the other side of the riverbed, is Funchal's famous ★★ **Market Hall** (*Mercado dos Lavradores*) ⑫. The former facade of the building has a blue-and-white tiled *azulejos* depiction of *Leda and the Swan*; and the market traders surround it, selling flowers, fruit and fish. Women dressed in typical Madeiran folkwear can be seen at the entrance, selling orchids, Bird of Paradise flowers, flamingo flowers and calla lilies – all of which can be securely packed and taken home by plane. There is also a picturesque arrangement of wicker baskets containing exotic fruit and vegetables, grouped around the inner court-yard on two levels. Space here is at a real premium on Friday and Saturday, when the farmers arrive from the country areas to sell their wares (Market Hall: Monday 7am–2pm, Tuesday to Thursday and Saturday 7am–4pm, Friday 7am–8pm).

*Home produce*

The narrow streets of the **Old Town** (*Zona Velha*) begin just beyond the rear of the Market Hall, where the fish is laid out for sale on long tables; this is a good place to stroll around and peer into the tiny stores and workshops. A more direct route is to turn right down the Rua Boa Vigem and then continue along the edge of the Old Town as far as a small pedestrian precinct. There's a pleasant little park here with fountains and benches, and old men can often be seen playing cards beneath the trees. The houses in this precinct have been restored, and there are several restaurants with chairs outside. The side streets contain pubs, and there's even a degree of nightlife.

*Corpo Santo chapel*

**29**

Beyond the pub area, things get a lot quieter. The old fishermen's **chapel of Corpo Santo** comes into view now, with its tiny basalt campanile. Walk through this peaceful residential area with its simple one-storey houses until the 17th-century ★ **Fortress of São Tiago** ⑬ appears, considered to be one of the finest in Portugal; its round towers with their domes and its ochre-coloured walls are anything but forbidding. The building is open to the public, and can be entered via the baroque gate. There is an excellent view from the terrace on the roof, and the fortress also houses the **Funchal Museum of Contemporary Art**, with its interesting collection of works by Portuguese artists spanning the last four decades (Monday to Friday 10am–12.30pm and 2–5.30pm).

*Fortress of São Tiago*

Go down the narrow street to the right now, passing some blue-and-white striped fishermen's huts, to reach the **Praia das Estrelas**. The few fishermen left in Funchal keep their little open boats on the pebble beach. Today, fishing is a spare-time activity for many of them; on Sundays they can often be seen sitting together mending their nets. The local population frequently comes here in the summer to swim.

Not far away and slightly higher up the hill to the left is the church of the Old Town, **Igreja do Socorro** ⑭. The interior contains some magnificent altars decorated with gold, and the wooden ceiling has several baroque paintings of saints. The original church on this site was built in the 16th century and consecrated to the Apostle Jacob, who was believed to have saved Funchal from an outbreak of the plague. After the 1748 earthquake it was completely rebuilt in the baroque style.

*Taking the plunge at Barreirinha*

*Typical balcony in the Old Town*

*Patricio & Gouveia:*
*handmade quality*

The new swimming centre known as **Barreirinha** lies beneath the nearby *Miradouro* (observation point). The sea can be reached easily via a flight of steps, and there is also a smaller pool for children. A snack bar, a restaurant, several changing cabins and toilet facilities all add to the comfort. A lift is to be installed to facilitate access down to the centre (8.30am–7pm).

Carry on back towards the Market Hall. The cobbles in the streets around here tend to be quite bumpy, so high heels aren't a good idea. More pubs and restaurants appear now; washing often flutters from lines on the tiny balconies; caged songbirds can sometimes be heard singing; and the tiled roofs are covered with common houseleek. Small children can frequently be seen playing barefoot at the edge of the road, door-knockers begin to outnumber doorbells, and the houses smell mustily of wood and mysterious spices. Mothers scolding, men gesticulating, and noisy workshops – the Old Town of Funchal is all of these things.

The city possesses several embroidery factories, and the most famous of them, ★ **Patricio & Gouveia** ⓯, isn't far from the Market Hall. This factory is a much better place to buy embroidered goods than the souvenir shops, as everything is guaranteed handmade. It's worth resisting the attractions of the sales rooms for a few moments, however, to take a brief look at the factory floor itself. Even the stairwell, with its squeaky steps and the old-fashioned lift, looks as if it belongs in a museum. On the second floor there's a strong smell of paint, and piled high against the wall are countless patterned rolls of material ready for embroidering; the patterns have been stencilled on to the material with blue dye by the women who work here. One floor higher up is the final stage in the process: the dye gets washed out of the embroidered material, which is carefully cleaned and ironed. A leaden seal is then added as proof of the product's authenticity.

Outside, the riverbed is covered with a profusion of violet-red bougainvillea. The weird-looking plant with inviting-looking branches just where the park begins is a dracena palm, also known as a dragon tree; this particularly fine specimen gets festooned with coloured lights at Christmas time. Just beyond the park, at the petrol station, turn off to the left down another avenue of rosewood trees. Here, far away from the beaten tourist track, is the ★ **Henrique e Francisco Franco Museum** ⓰. The building itself is fascinating, with its temple-like appearance and pillared entrance, and it houses the work of the two artist brothers. Henrique Franco (1883–1961) was the less well-known of the two; his Madeiran landscapes have a real warmth to them, and he also did a series of portraits, taking farming families and young women as his subjects. The works of his brother Francisco Franco (1885–1955) are far less conventional: he was a sculptor and worked with wood, clay and stone. His most famous works include the aviator's monument in Funchal harbour, and the bust of João Gonçalvez Zarco in Terreiro da Luta, both of them cast in bronze. Many of his smaller sculptures can also be admired in several of the island's museums. His charcoal sketches are very interesting too, and betray the influence of the Paris school (Monday to Friday 9am –12.30pm and 2–5.30pm).

The avenue now passes the bed of a stream, overgrown with flowers, and the Law Courts before arriving at the **Town Hall Square** (*Praça do Município*), the old heart of the city, which lies at some distance from today's centre. In the middle of the square, surrounded by splashing fountains, is a column with an armillary sphere at the top – a popular resting place for pigeons.

*The Town Hall Square*

The **Town Hall 🕜** can be recognised from the flags outside and the municipal coat of arms carved into its stone facade: the five sugar loaves awarded to the city by King Manuel in 1508 are clearly visible, as are the four wine grapes that were added later on. They represent the two former pillars of the island's industry. Funchal's town hall was built in 1758 by Count João José de Carvalhal, who at that time was the richest man on the island. He stored barrels of wine on the ground floor of the building (where he kept his horses), and lived with his family on the first floor. The enormous tower in the background with the broad windows served as a harbour look-out post, enabling the master of the house to keep an eye on arriving ships, so that he could get to the quay to do business far more quickly than most of his competitors. The count's family

31

*The inner courtyard of the Town Hall*

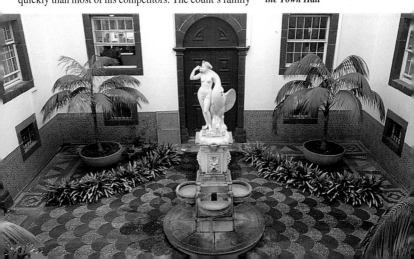

sold the building to the city around a century ago. The inner courtyard (public access during working hours), with its *azulejos* tiled walls and its fountain, is most attractive, and the gallery on the first floor provides access to the ★ **Civic Museum** (*Museu da Cidade*) which, though small, has a well arranged collection of exhibits documenting the history of Funchal (Monday to Friday 9am–noon and 2–5.30pm).

The main building dominating the Town Hall Square is the **Jesuit Seminary** ⓲. The Jesuits arrived on Madeira at the end of the 16th century ostensibly to comfort the population after the traumatic pirate raid of 1566, though they also made a handsome profit from the wine trade. The seminary was a place of education for the sons of noble families; today it houses the city's university. The baroque, 17th-century church is a lot more sober than its counterparts in, say, Rome, but it still has some interesting marble statues of Jesuit saints on its facade. The founder of the Jesuit Order, St Ignatius of Loyola, can be seen at the bottom left.

Another interesting building on the Town Hall Square, hidden away behind two oleander bushes opposite the seminary, is the 18th-century **Bishop's Palace**. With its arcaded passageway and low gallery on the first floor, it is a lot less spectacular, however. Access to the building is from the Rua do Bispo behind it. The palace houses the ★ **Museum of Ecclesiastical Art** (*Museu de Arte Sacra*)

*Exhibits in the Museum of Ecclesiastical Art*

⓳. Its impressive collection of Flemish oil paintings was acquired by the island in return for sugar imports during the 15th and 16th centuries, and many of the works originally adorned Madeira's village churches and private chapels. There are also a few Flemish wooden statues as well as several more recent works, such as figurines of saints by Portuguese artists, most of them also carved in the Flemish style. The highlight of the collection of church treasure here is a processional cross 1.2m (4ft) high, presented to Funchal Cathedral by King Manuel I at the beginning of the 16th century.

Leave the square, with its semicircular patterns of black-and-white cobblestones, and head down the Rua das Pretas towards the upper part of town. The word *pretas* means 'negresses' and dates back to the time of slavery on Madeira, when blacks were forced to live in ghettoes which they were not allowed to leave at night. Most of Funchal's antiques shops can be found around here. Squeezed between two houses at the end of the street is the 16th-century **Igreja de São Pedro**, with its magnificent baroque interior. To the left of the church, at the beginning of the Rua da Moraria (where the Moorish slaves used to live), there is an interesting town house which, like

*Igreja de São Pedro: the high altar*

the Town Hall, used to belong to the Carvalhal family: it now contains the **Municipal Museum** (*Museu Municipal*). The exhibits include an aquarium on the ground floor and stuffed animals on the upper ones; most interesting is the building itself with its elegant roofed-over inner courtyard, double staircase and dark wooden fittings.

Now steel yourself for a climb. A narrow street without any protecting pavement leads steeply upwards to one of the real highlights of this tour, the ★★ **Quinta das Cruzes** ❷⓿. Legend has it that João Gonçalvez Zarco lived here during the 15th century; all that remains today of the original structure are just a few foundation walls. Like so many other buildings in Funchal, the present one was rebuilt in baroque style after it was damaged during the earthquake of 1748. It is surrounded by a beautiful park, which is hidden behind high walls and hardly visible from the street.

*More sacred art in Quinta das Cruzes*

The park contains a small archaeological area consisting of sections of masonry and stonework taken from a number of Funchal's buildings that have since been demolished. Heraldic emblems carved in stone, gravestones, fonts from churches and basalt crosses form just part of this fascinating collection. Perhaps the most interesting exhibit is a fragment of the city's former pillory, which once stood on the Largo do Pelourinho; today a copy stands on the site (*see page 28*). Two more important exhibits can be seen lying some distance away under the trees and overgrown with ivy: a pair of massive window frames with imaginative and elaborate carvings of plants, demons and ship's ropes. They are among the finest examples of Manueline stonemasonry on Madeira, but their history is unclear. Most people think they were taken from the city's first hospital.

*Hide and seek in the park*

**33**

Previous owners of the house collected a large number of tropical plants from all kinds of different countries. Orchids are grown on the top floor of the building. Giant lady's slipper blooms in the park during winter and spring and there are also enormous tree ferns, ornamental bananas, Indian laurels, fuchsias, azaleas and a large dracena palm. The grounds of the Quinta das Cruzes have a special tranquillity of their own; not many tourists find their way up here, and a short spell on one of the benches is very restful.

The house contains a good **museum** (Tuesday to Sunday 10am–12.30pm and 2–6pm; park: daily 10am–6pm). On the ground floor to the right in Hall 12 there are several examples of so-called sugar-box furniture (*see pages 74–5*). Hall 14 has a collection of old tiles (*azulejos*) created according to an ancient technique whereby the surface was divided up into various sections to prevent the glaze from running.

Those with energy to spare should continue further up the hill. It's a tough climb as far as the next side-street to the left; at the end of it is a large gateway, where there's usually a small door left open for pedestrians to walk through and enter the tall, dark basalt walls of the **Fortaleza do Pico ㉑**. This grim and forbidding-looking building dates from the end of the 16th century; today it is part of a military base and is closed to visitors. The walk up here is more than worth it, however, for the fantastic view across the centre of Funchal. In the foreground are the high trees surrounding the Quinta das Cruzes, and beyond them the tiled dome of the convent church of Santa Clara and all the other highlights of any city tour. Up here they can all be contemplated at leisure before you stroll back down towards the centre (possibly stopping off at a café on the way for a well-earned break).

## Further sights

The ★ **Quinta Magnólia ㉒**, with its magnificent park, can be reached via Rua do Dr Pita and is above the Quinta do Sol hotel. Once the home of the British Country Club, this splendid mansion now belongs to the city of Funchal. The food here is good and is cooked and served up by the Funchal school of catering. The enormous trees in the grounds provide plenty of shade and include a magnificent bird of paradise tree – a relative of the flower. The park also has tennis courts, a swimming pool, and a keep-fit trail in the nearby ravine – all free of charge.

*Afternoon tea at Reid's*

★ **Reid's Hotel ㉓**, not far from the Quinta Magnólia on the Estrada Monumental, is a very noble establishment. It was once ranked among the top hotels in the world. Today it has lost some of its former glory but it is still a cut above the standard tourist hotel, with its beautiful gardens and superb views. Afternoon tea on the terrace overlooking the sea is extremely pleasant.

*Bird of paradise*

The hotel was founded by the Reids, a Scottish family whose estate (*Quinta de Bom Sucesso*) is now the city's ★ **Botanical Garden** (*Jardim Botânico*). The old mansion itself houses a small **Natural History Museum**. The Botanical Garden contains a magnificent collection of orchids and numerous other tropical and subtropical plants, and one section is devoted to plants native to Madeira. There is an excellent view of Funchal Bay from the terrace of the café, or from the nearby observation platforms. Fountains, lily-ponds and birdsong make the whole park quite idyllic.

On top of the next hill is the ★★ **Orchid Garden** (*Jardim Orqídea*), which is certainly worth a visit. It was lovingly

laid out below the Botanical Garden by an Austrian couple, and contains some of the rarest orchids in the world, all of them 'home-grown'. A look inside the laboratory is instructive in this regard: the sensitive plants spend their first few years in test tubes, being fed precise amounts of nutrients while being bathed in ultraviolet light. They are only allowed out into natural light and air after four years or so, and it takes several more years after that for the first blossom to appear (daily 9am–6pm).

*Enjoying Madeira's flora*
*A rare orchid*

## Excursions

★★★ **Monte**, Funchal's villa area, lies high above the city, just below the cloud layer. Numerous wealthy individuals have settled here since the last century, and many live in *quintas* with magnificent parks around them. The centre of the municipality is the area around the church. The road passes an **ivy-covered bridge**, once part of the funicular railway that travelled to Monte and on to Terreiro da Luta higher up. There was a serious accident on this line at the end of the 1930s, after which journeys were suspended for good. During World War II the rails were torn up and sold to mainland Portugal. Today most people are sad that the charming old funicular railway no longer exists; access to Monte is by coach and car.

*Ivy-covered bridge, Monte*

The yellow building on the Largo do Monte is the former railway station, and the terrace of the nearby **Café do Parque** is a good place for a relatively quiet drink; quite often an accordion player wearing Madeiran folk dress will sit down on a bench close by and start serenading the guests. The marble fountain here, known as the Fonte do Largo, is considered sacred and is always covered with flowers and candles.

A flight of steps paved with basalt leads up steeply to the pilgrimage church of ★ **Nossa Senhora do Monte**. Construction work on the building was carried out at great

*Accordion welcome at Café do Parque*

*Nossa Senhora do Monte: the miraculous vision and interior*

expense during the 18th century. Legend has it that in the 15th century, a young shepherd girl from Terreiro da Luta saw the Virgin Mary in a vision. She ran home to tell her parents, who were not convinced. When the girl continued to have visions her father secretly followed her to see whether she was telling the truth. Although he failed to see the Virgin, he did find a statue of the Madonna and a chapel was built in her honour on the site of to-day's church. The Virgin of Monte has been accorded great reverence ever since. To the left of the entrance portal there is an *azulejos* picture depicting the girl's miraculous vision; the original statue is extremely small and is kept in a small silver shrine at the main altar.

A side chapel to the left, built during the 1960s, contains the tomb of the last emperor of Austria, Karl I (Charles IV of Hungary), who died in exile on Madeira. The amount of wreaths and floral gifts around the simple metal coffin demonstrates how many Austrians still come here to honour the grave of their last monarch. At the end of World War I, Karl von Habsburg was forced to abdicate, and spent the first part of his exile in Switzerland. From there he made several attempts to preserve at least the Hungarian throne for himself, but all were in vain. He was placed under arrest by the victorious powers and then taken on a British warship to Madeira, where he and his wife Zita arrived in 1921. He lived in an old villa in Monte for several months before dying of pneumonia on 1 April 1922.

Steps lead down to a small terrace in front of the church, and when going down try to visualise the faithful sliding down them on their knees, as they do on 15 August every year during the big pilgrimage here. When the rivers in Funchal burst their banks during a heavy rainstorm in 1803 and caused a lot of damage to life and property, the people begged the Virgin of Monte for help. The rain

*Nossa Senhora do Monte*

stopped and the Virgin was henceforth declared patron saint of the island; one year later this was officially confirmed by the Pope. Ever since that time, the pilgrimage on Assumption Day has been the most important church festival on the island. People arrive in Funchal from all over Madeira, and the colourful procession is followed in the early evening by fireworks, music and all kinds of entertainment.

From the terrace there's a good view of Monte's main attraction, the famous ★★★ **wickerwork sleds** (*Carros de Cesto*), waiting for tourists eager to travel down to Livramento or even as far as Funchal. The sleds, which are surprisingly comfortable, have wooden skids and each one is operated by two men in white shirts, white trousers and straw boaters. This exhilarating experience mustn't be missed. The sleds were first introduced in 1849 after horses and carts had proved unable to cope with the steep route up to Monte. The new vehicles, probably unique, became a tourist attraction almost overnight. The Urals in Russia are said to have something similar, but with wheels rather than skids. Each sled has room for two or three passengers, and these days they don't need to be dragged back up to Monte by hand: a lorry does the job instead. The men controlling the sled don't mind the hard work at all, since they earn a lot in tips.

*Taking the quick way down*

**37**

Before your gravity-powered toboggan ride, it's worth taking a short stroll through the pretty park that lies between the church and the route formerly taken by the funicular. Ferns, camellias, oak trees and palm trees all grow quite happily alongside each other up here, and in springtime the magnolia blossom is splendid.

Just a few steps below the wickerwork-sled station, down a steep section of road, is another magnificent park, the ★ **Jardim do Monte** (Monday to Friday 9am–5pm). The entrance price is almost as steep as the road here, but it's more than justified. This enormous park, which doesn't usually get too many visitors, used to belong to the Monte Palace Hotel, which during the early years of this century was considered one of the best in Funchal. After World War II it fell into disrepair but was then bought and restored by José Berardo, a Madeiran who had made his fortune in South Africa.

*Jardim do Monte*

Today the villa lies at the centre of a park which has not only kept its old trees but also contains numerous new botanical specialities. There is a comprehensive collection of palm ferns (*cycas*) here, which Berardo had specially imported from South Africa. He also filled the gardens with all manner of eccentric objects, including old pieces of stonemasonry and *azulejos* tile pictures from mainland Portugal. There are Chinese vases, valuable pieces of crystal and pieces of petrified wood, too.

*Statue in the gardens*

*Tiles in the Japanese Garden*

*The Curral Valley*

*Weaving willow, Curral*

Walk up the small valley along the stream as far as the ★ **Japanese garden** where the entrance is guarded by marble lions. There are statues of fantastic figures, tiny red temples, copies of pagodas, azaleas and water everywhere in grottoes and fountains. Anyone wondering how a Japanese garden comes to be on Madeira will find the answer in the upper section of the garden on the colourful tiled wall, where the history of Portuguese relations with Japan from the early 16th century to the present is illustrated in words and pictures. The large tile picture is a contemporary work, designed by Alberto Cedrón and produced in a Lisbon workshop.

The road to ★ **Curral das Freiras** first winds its way up to **Pico dos Barcelos**, an observation point on the western edge of Funchal. The way up to the viewing terrace is often lined with souvenir sellers peddling hand-knitted pullovers and similar items. Despite that, there's a magnificent view across Funchal from the top. A bumpy road then leads up steeply through eucalyptus forest along the upper slopes of the Curral Valley. Livestock breeders often herd their goats into the forests up here, and forest fires are sometimes deliberately lit to get the trees to germinate afresh. A roadsign points the way to Eira do Serrado. This brief detour leads to a car park with yet more souvenir salesmen; there's a little bar here too. A ten-minute walk along a path leads up to the ★ *miradouro*, where there's a particularly good view across the **Curral Valley** and the town of Curral das Freiras far below. Those without a head for heights shouldn't get too close to the parapet, because this observation point really is perched, vertically, around 800m (2,600ft) above the valley below.

A dimly lit tunnel leads down into the valley basin of Curral das Freiras. Hairpin bends take you into the centre of the town, which is situated on a small rise in the middle of the valley and boasts two or three restaurants, a few pubs and souvenir shops and, a little further down, the 19th-century church of Nossa Senhora do Livramento. The farmers of Curral have lined the whole valley most impressively with thousands of *poios* – tiny terraced fields where they grow wine, fruit and vegetables. White willows grow on the moist valley floor and chestnut trees up on the slopes. Curral das Freiras is famous for its chestnut-flavoured soups and cakes and its chestnut liqueur. It even holds its own annual Chestnut Festival after the harvest on 1 November.

The name Curral das Freiras literally means 'Hideaway of the Nuns', and the town owes its odd name to when the French pirates attacked Funchal in 1566. The nuns from Funchal's Convent of Santa Clara escaped and hid there until the pirates had left.

## Route 2

*Machico*

### ★★ Machico

With its population of around 20,000, Machico, the first
capital of Madeira, is the island's second largest town, but
for five centuries it has been a sleepy little provincial back-
water. Today Machico is gradually starting to wake up:
there's been quite an economic upswing here in recent
years, caused mainly by tourism. Hotels and a large bungalow area on the outskirts of the town have now been followed by restaurants, cafés and shops.

### History

Legend has it that the town of Machico was named after
an Englishman, Robert Machim, who was shipwrecked
here along with his mistress, Anna d'Arfet, in 1344. The
two of them survived the ordeal but died of exposure
only a few weeks later. They were buried under a cedar
tree by survivors of their ship's crew, who then set sail
in a makeshift raft. Captured by Moorish pirates, the sailors
told their story in Morocco and eventually it reached the
ears of King John of Portugal. The king related the story
of Machim to his sons, one of whom was to become Henry
the Navigator. His naval commander Zarco eventually
landed on Madeira, and is said to have found the grave.

After the islands were claimed by the Portuguese,
Machico was regarded as Madeira's joint capital, along
with Funchal, and ruled the island's eastern half until 1497.

### Sights

Begin the tour of the town at the **Cais** , Machico's little quay, where João Gonçalvez Zarco is supposed to have
first arrived with his crew. Today the odd fishing vessel
can often be seen chugging by, and the view from here

*Fishing off the Cais*

*Fishing boat under construction*

*Swimming off the quay*

*Capela dos Milagres:*
*column detail*

40

extends across the whole of Machico Bay with its pebble beach, taking in the boatyard where the wooden fishing boats are built and, far off to the left, the Dom Pedro Hotel – the town's tallest building.

High above is the **Fortress of São João Batista ❷**, built at the beginning of the 18th century as a defence against pirates. Later it was used as a hospital, and today it provides accommodation for so-called *retornados* – men who came to Portugal from its former colonies after they were given independence in the mid-1970s. Many of them have failed to find a real foothold here even now.

Follow the road along the edge of the harbour and into the town itself. During the afternoon, fishermen can usually be seen repairing their long rods, which they place between two plane trees. The lines are up to 2,000m (6,500ft) long and are used to catch a Madeiran speciality, the *espada* or cutlass fish (*see page 81*). The flat wooden constructions above the road are for drying *gaiado*, a small variety of tuna.

In the square known as the Largo dos Milagres, pleasantly shaded by tall Indian laurel trees, is the ★ **Chapel of Miracles** (*Capela dos Milagres*) ❸, whose predecessor on the same site is thought to have been commissioned by Zarco himself in around 1425. The building was destroyed by fire in the 16th century, and yet again by floods in 1803. The present structure dates from 1815. A plaque next to the entrance shows that on 5 November 1956 the level of the Machico River was also dangerously high. The chapel contains the famous wooden statue of the Lord of Miracles (*Senhor dos Milagres*). During the floods of

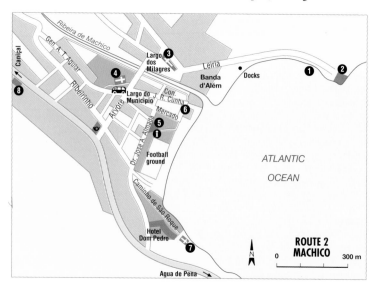

ROUTE 2
MACHICO

1803, the statue was washed out to sea and miraculously discovered by an American sailor, who rowed it ashore from his ship anchored out in Machico Bay. The incident is depicted on an oil painting hanging to the left of the altar. The picture to the right gives a good impression of what the area surrounding the chapel must have looked like during the last century.

The miracle is celebrated every year in Machico with a large festival held on the evening of 8 October, when pilgrims from all over the island come to the town to pray for themselves or their friends to be healed from all kinds of diseases. During the procession they carry wax effigies of the various bodily parts they want cured.

The part of Machico on the eastern bank of the river is known as Banda d'Além, which used to be the town's fishing quarter. A bridge, with cows grazing peacefully beneath it, leads to the actual centre of the town. To the left of the town hall there is a modern 20th-century structure; more interesting, though, is the church of ★ **Nossa Senhora da Conceição ❹**. Built in around 1500 and consecrated to Our Lady of the Immaculate Conception, it is one of the oldest buildings in the town. In the square in front of the church is a monument to Tristão Vaz Teixeira, co-founder of the island in 1419 along with Zarco. After the island was divided up into two fiefs, Vaz Teixeira was given the eastern part with Machico as its capital. After his death, his son and his uncle continued to rule, and it was only at the end of the 15th century that Funchal was declared sole capital of Madeira. The side portal of the church, with its three marble pillars, was a gift from King Manuel I. Enter the church through the main portal, which features several good examples of Manueline stonemasonry decoration. Grotesque faces can still be seen on the left of the entrance, and are meant to represent evil; the stone on the right-hand side is too weathered now for the 'good' to be properly made out.

As with so many other churches on the island, the interior was radically altered during the baroque period; the altar with its gold leaf decoration and the coffered ceiling both date from that time. Two of the side chapels on the left still survive from the Manueline period. One of them contains the blue coat of arms of the Vaz Teixeira family, depicting a phoenix rising from the ashes; several members of the family are thought to be interred beneath the wooden floor.

Outside the church, walk in the direction of the sea along the narrow street opposite the church. ★ **House No 15** is particularly interesting: its display window contains ancient wine bottles covered with cobwebs and dust, and some of these vintages date back to 1842 to the days

*Nossa Senhora da Conceição*

**41**

*Interior with gold leaf decoration*

*Old Madeira wine at No 15*

*Boatbuilders taking a break*

before the phylloxera crisis. These bottles are almost priceless today, of course – despite the fact that vast stocks of Madeira wine, personally ordered by Catherine the Great, were recently discovered in the Kremlin.

On the right a few steps further on is the former site of Machico's old market (a tile next to the entrance actually still bears the inscription *Mercado Velho*). There was a restaurant here with old-fashioned tables and chairs grouped around the fountain in the middle, but unfortunately it was destroyed in a fire quite recently. The ochre-coloured building without any windows directly opposite is the **Fortress of Nossa Senhora do Amparo ⑤**. It was built in 1706, and owes its existence to a governor of the island who decided to put a stop to the threat of pirate attack once and for all: Machico was given three fortresses, only two of which still survive, so that pirate ships could be attacked from all sides if they entered the bay. An interesting feature of the Amparo fortress is its triangular shape, which enabled its cannon to be pointed seawards on two sides. A look-out up on the nearby Pico do Facho, east of the town (recognisable by the radio mast on the top), gave the alarm the moment pirate ships appeared on the horizon. Today the fortress contains a tourist information bureau.

Back down on the seafront are the three open halls of the **Lota ⑥**, where freshly caught fish – mainly Tuna – is auctioned. Follow the harbour promenade in the direction of the Dom Pedro Hotel. The small chapel at the end of the promenade, the **Capela de São Roque ⑦**, contains several valuable baroque tile pictures showing scenes from the life of St Roche, but the building is unfortunately nearly always closed. The Spring of St Roche lies below the chapel; the water comes straight out of the rock and is popular with the locals, who believe it cures all manner of ailments. Continue uphill along the main street that leads from the Dom Pedro Hotel in the direction of Portela and Caniçal; on the left 450m (500yd) further on is the ★ **Casa das Bordadeiras de Machico ⑧**, where hand-embroidered goods can be purchased. The building looks a bit grim from the outside, but it's still worth a visit since the wares sold here are totally authentic. A small, narrow flight of stairs leads up to the first floor. The embroidered material is carefully cleaned, stored and sold by the women who work in the three tiny rooms up here.

On the coast road west of Machico lies the village of **Agua de Pena**, with its luxury hotel and its large bungalow area. Agua de Pena has virtually become Machico's 'hotel region': there is a small swimming area by the sea that can be reached via a steep flight of steps. The centre of Machico is just 15 minutes away from here on foot.

# Route 3

**Funchal – Blandy's Garden – Camacha – Porto da Cruz – Machico – Ponta de São Lourenço – Santa Cruz – Caniço (90km/55 miles)** *See map on page 44*

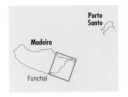

This route from Funchal begins by crossing the low mountain range in the east of the island. This region gets quite a bit of rain, and the vegetation is correspondingly lush. The roads are lined with hydrangeas and agapanthus blossom; the blooms in Blandy's Garden are exceptionally magnificent. In Camacha, a wickerwork shop is definitely worth a visit, and a detour to the north coast takes in the wine area around Porto da Cruz. The journey then continues through the Machico Valley as far as the Ponta de São Lourenço, the desolate easternmost point of Madeira with its bizarre rock formations. After a quick visit to the historic centre of Santa Cruz, the route then returns back along the coast to Funchal. The entire trip can easily be done in a day by hire car or taxi. Those intending to travel by local bus should plan an overnight stay at Santo da Serra, Machico or Caniçal.

*Blandy's blooms*

43

To the east of Funchal the road ascends steeply towards ★★ **Blandy's Garden** (Quinta do Palheiro Ferreiro). After paying admission at the gate, walk down the camellia-lined avenue as far as the Blandy family **mansion**, built in the colonial style at the upper end of the park at the end of the 19th century. Its grounds are extremely well tended, and the Blandys – once the richest family on the island – had an excellent view of them from their windows. Innumerable plants from all over the world, and especially from subtropical countries, can be found here. Even botanists have a hard time distinguishing them all. The

*Blandy's Garden*

*Wickerwork wonders in Camacha*

*The lily pond*

*Agapanthus*

podraneas growing in one corner were brought from South Africa by the present owner's mother. The 'sunken garden' beneath the mansion was laid out in French style; its symmetrical hedges have been trimmed into several fantastic shapes. Water lilies bloom on a small pond at the centre. Lupins and star-of-Bethlehem, azaleas and rhododendrons cover the banks of the small stream that flows through the gardens. The small baroque chapel dates from the time when Count Carvalhal used the garden as a hunting preserve around 200 years ago. A covered arcade adorned with blossom leads to the 'Lady's Garden', also laid out in the French style, with some of its hedges cut into unusual shapes. The blossom here is particularly magnificent, and there is a good view across the nearby golf course. An iron gate provides access to the grounds of the old mansion, commissioned by Count Carvalhal, which has remained uninhabited ever since the Blandy family bought the estate. Its walls shimmer romantically between the tall trees. (Monday to Friday 9.30am–12.30pm)

The road to Camacha is lined with orchards. There are tree ferns next to the houses, and in spring the apple blossom contrasts magnificently with the azaleas and camellias. Later, in summer, the blue blossom of the agapanthus is a characteristic feature. The centre of ★ **Camacha** (pop. 6,500), 10km (6 miles), lies on a flat mountain ridge sloping steeply down to the southeast coast. An observation point (*miradouro*) high above the sea affords a magnificent view of eucalyptus forests and terraced fields. Next

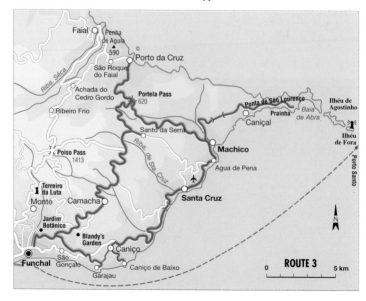

to this is Camacha's most famous sight, the ★ **Café Reló-gio**, with its eye-catching clocktower which looks as if it was modelled on Big Ben, because the first owners were a wealthy English family who used it as a summer residence in the 19th century. Today the building is the headquarters of the largest wicker goods export company on Madeira. The sales rooms contain shelves and shelves of wicker products of all types, ranging from simple baskets to cane furniture. There is also a fascinating collection of wickerwork animals, which are not for sale because no one knows how they were made. Beneath the basement floor is the workshop where the basket makers can be observed at work; the technique is difficult, and they are not particularly well paid. Only a fraction of the wares on display in the Café Relógio comes from here; most were created in family homes across the island.

In 1875 a very important historical event occurred on the square in front of the Café Relógio: a plaque records the proud fact that the first ever football match on Portuguese soil was played there. An Englishman who was living in Camacha had brought a football back and he organised a proper game.

The road now continues in the direction of Santo da Serra along a seemingly endless stretch of winding road, leading through small hamlets where farmers grow fruit and vegetables. Slightly above the road is thick forest: this is where the cloud layer starts, and the land higher up is too damp for agricultural purposes. Small white willows, which are harvested in March or April, can be seen down on the valley floor: many farmers in this region earn their living selling osier to the wicker workshops on Camacha.

In **Santo da Serra**, 21km (13 miles), a visit to the ★★ **Quinta do Santa da Serra** is essential. There's a large car park behind the church, close to the town centre. A

*Fresh vegetables on the road to Santo da Serra*

**45**

*Camacha basketry*

cobbled path lined with white azaleas leads up to the grounds of the *quinta*. Spring is a good time to visit because of the camellias; in summer the hydrangeas are in bloom. The pink-coloured mansion, once the property of the Blandy family, lies half-hidden behind enormous, lichen-covered trees. Today the house and grounds are state-owned. The Quinta do Santa da Serra is a favourite weekend destination for the locals, who come here to enjoy the sports grounds, play areas and even a small zoo. Follow the cobbled path to the rear section of the gardens as far as the ★ **Miradouro dos Ingleses**, which has a fantastic view of eastern Madeira. A look-out used to stand here and report to the head of the Blandy family whenever trading vessels came into view on the horizon, whereupon Mr Blandy, a wine trader, would set off for Funchal as quickly as possible to negotiate his business.

Santo da Serra has a golf course – the first one ever laid out on Madeira. It has 18 holes at present, but will soon have 27. The course is just outside the town and can be reached by continuing down the road past park of Santo da Serra. Opposite the golf course, on a small rise, a natural crater lake has been converted into a large reservoir. Halfway between the park and the golf course, the former golf club building can be seen at the roadside. It has lain disused for several years now. Built around the turn of the century, this attractive building has a colourful art nouveau tiled frieze on its small tower.

Now it's not far to **Portela**, 26km (16 miles), a small community of just a few houses which marks the watershed between the south and north of the island; the weather can start getting decidedly damp beyond Santo da Serra. Life in this region during the winter is tough, and it's easy to understand why the traditional woollen hat with earmuffs known as the *Barrete de Lã* is still popular with the men. There's a well-known adage attached to these hats: apparently during the day the earmuffs are worn in the raised position, but are lowered at night after their owners have had a few beers, to block out their wives' nosy questions about where the money went...

The Casa de Portela restaurant, famed for its giant pieces of skewered meat (*espetadas*), lies at the head of the **Portela Pass**. The meat is served with a wine from nearby Porto da Cruz, with an aftertaste reminiscent of blackberries. There's a good view of Porto da Cruz from the Portela Pass – the houses can be seen spread thinly across the narrow mountain ridge leading down to the north coast and more densely packed together right next to the sea. Beyond is the steep **Eagle Rock** (*Penha de Aguia*), the symbol of northern Madeira. This enormous, 590-m (1,935-ft) high rock is almost inaccessible and can only be scaled along narrow paths.

*Hats to cover the ears*

*Eagle rock*

Those with time on their hands could take a brief detour at this point from the Portela Pass to **Porto da Cruz**, 6km (4 miles) away. This small town doesn't have much to offer, apart from the small cemetery on the outskirts with its typically Portuguese metal crosses, photographs and vast amount of flowers. There are two beaches, both of them pebbly and too dangerous for swimming, but the pounding waves and spray are really magnificent to see. One of the few remaining sugar mills on Madeira stands on the promontory between the two beaches. Between March and May, after the harvest, rum is produced here; the rest of the time, the building is deserted.

The route now continues east along the **Machico Valley**. The road is lined with acacias, and the blossom in spring is a marvellous pale yellow. At the mouth of the river lies Machico (*see pages 39–42*).

Carrying on northwards along the coast towards Caniçal, it's worth looking out across the Machico Valley, with its numerous small terraced fields. A lot of sugar cane used to be grown here, but those days are over and only a few fields remain, providing just enough cane for the sugar mill at Porto da Cruz to make the rum. The road now goes through a tunnel, and emerges into a different world entirely. Suddenly the landscape is dry, the fields have disappeared, and the road is lined with palm trees.

**Caniçal** (pop. 3,300), 43km (26 miles), is a small fishing community. Before the tunnel was built in the 1950s and the village was given its own *levada* connection, agriculture here was out of the question; apart from a small amount of dairy farming, the inhabitants had concentrated mainly on fishing. Today Caniçal still boasts a large fishing fleet, consisting of small open boats as well as larger tuna-fish cutters. They lie at anchor down in the bay unless the weather is rough, in which case they are pulled up on to the stony beach. There is even a small boatyard here where they can be repaired. The small cafés around the harbour are a good place to sit and soak up the sun whenever the rest of the island is cloudy.

Caniçal's **Whaling Museum** (*Museu da Baleia*) (Tuesday to Friday 10am–noon and 1–5pm; Saturday, Sunday and public holidays 10am–noon and 1–6pm) is not far from the harbour; its undisputed highlight is the life-size model of a sperm whale. The contrast in size between the mammal itself and the tiny whaling boat beside it conveys a vivid impression of the risks involved. Photographs depict the old method of whaling, with lance and harpoon. Whaling around Madeira has been banned since 1982, and the sperm whale is now a strictly protected species. Small wooden models of whaling boats and also carved pieces of whalebone can be purchased at a small souvenir stand.

*Cow byre in the Machico Valley*

*Carefree days in Caniçal*

*Memory of a bygone age*

*Ponta de São Lourenço*

*Local encounter*

A large free-trade zone (*Zona Franca*) was set up to the east of Caniçal in the hope of attracting foreign investors and creating jobs for the Machico/Caniçal region. Several years have gone by since then, and only three local firms from Funchal have taken advantage of the opportunity. Large areas have been flattened by bulldozers, but not much has been constructed so far. The new harbour at Caniçal is largely unused, though it does provide useful shelter for the local fishing boats during rough weather.

From Caniçal the road continues out to the ★★ **Ponta de São Lourenço**, 48km (29 miles), the easternmost point of Madeira, and ends at the Baia de Abra, from where it's possible to continue on foot along a narrow path to the tip of the point. The walk there and back takes about three hours. The lighthouse visible from the Baia de Abra can't be reached on foot, as it actually stands on an island off the coast. This peninsula was once covered in forest, but the trees were chopped down centuries ago and the area was used as pastureland for goats, so the trees never grew back. Now a nature reserve, it is hoped that the original vegetation will gradually regenerate. In early spring the peninsula becomes a sea of flowers but in summer it is dry and bare. On a clear day, there's a wonderful view of the three uninhabited islands known as the **Desertas**.

*The Desertas*

On the way back along the peninsula it's worth stopping at the **Prainha**, Madeira's only natural sandy beach, where there's a restaurant and several picnic sites. Nearby is a small extinct volcano with the pretty **Capela da Senhora da Piedade** at its summit. A procession is held to this chapel on the third weekend in every September.

The wind generators visible along the ridge of the peninsula provide Caniçal and the adjacent free trade area with energy. Wind energy accounts for 6.5 percent of Madeira's overall energy consumption.

The route now follows the coast southwards via Machico to Agua de Pena. At this point a massive pillared construction comes into view, which is the airport's runway extension, opened in 1985; the airport on Madeira used to have a reputation for being extremely dangerous. The locals still refer to this construction ironically as 'the aircraft carrier'. The coast road runs directly beneath the mighty concrete roof, supported by enormous pillars.

Continue on past the airport buildings to **Santa Cruz** (pop. 10,000), 69km (42 miles). This town's proximity to the airport has hindered tourist development, which is a shame because Santa Cruz is a rewarding place for a short stay. The pebble beach is lined with large palm trees and colourful fishing boats lie between them. The small park behind the harbour is a good place to relax, and has a post-modern café in the middle with comfortable seating.

*Palm trees at Santa Cruz*

Not far away is the town's ★ **market hall**, famous for its fresh fish. The large tiled frieze at the entrance by the Portuguese artist Outeiro Agueda is quite remarkable: it depicts fishermen and fishmongers, women sowing and farmers ploughing. A little further on is the new bathing centre of Praia das Palmeiras with its changing cabins, toilet facilities and a swimming pool, guarded by a bizarre-looking model of a sperm whale, and a lovely view of the nearby dragon trees.

*Modern art at the market hall*

At the centre of the town is the square – or rather triangle – known as the Praceta, lined with shops. The church of ★ **São Salvador**, with its defending tower, stands some distance away from the sea. It was built in 1533, and the whitewashed buttresses flanking the entrance are remarkable. The main portal, the rose window and the small portal facing the parvis all have stone carvings dating from the Manueline era. This three-aisled building is the largest church on the island outside Funchal.

*São Salvador church*

Inside, the aisles are separated by Gothic pointed arches. Hardly any alterations were made during the baroque period due to lack of money, which fortunately means that much of this Manueline structure remained unchanged. The window adjacent to the main portal with its crucifix of the Order of the Cross dates from the Manueline era, as does the small double portal separating altar and sacristy. The stone tomb on the left-hand wall, guarded by two mythical creatures, is believed to be even older; many consider it to have come from a previous building on the site, and it has been dated to around 1470. The massive slab of slate set into the pavement of the choir was especially imported from Flanders; it covers the tomb of the church's founder, João de Freitas. The sacristy contains several excellent examples of 16th-century *azulejos* tile work from Seville, taken from a former Franciscan monastery near Santa Cruz.

On the opposite side of the church square is the early 16th-century **Town Hall**; its two double-arched windows on the first floor, and the portal bearing the Portuguese coat of arms is disticly Manueline in style. Close by is another magnificent Madeiran park, with its flowerbeds shaded by massive Indian laurels.

Inland, the town of **Caniço** (pop. 8,000), 80km (49 miles) centres around the 18th-century parish church, consecrated to the Holy Ghost as well as to St Anthony of Padua, as the plaque above the portal demonstrates. At one stage there were two parishes in Caniço, separated by a stream. When both churches needed renovation, the decision was made to create a single parish. The facade of the remaining church is baroque, and a black-and-white mosaic leads to the entrance. The interior is unpretentious: the altars are painted white, and decorated only sparingly with gold leaf.

The locals meet up in the church square, and although tourism plays an important role in the suburbs of Caniço de Baixa and Garajau on the coast, life in the middle of town remains traditional, with hardly a tourist in sight.

However, what is perhaps the most idyllic holiday village in all of Madeira was recently built on the southern outskirts of Caniço, in the grounds of the ★ **Quinta Spléndida**, with its magnificent view out over the sea. The studios and apartments in the well-tended park surrounding this old mansion have successfully retained the architectural style of the original building.

*Quinta Spléndida*

A small road passes the Quinta Spléndida and leads down to ★ **Caniço de Baixa**, 3km (1¾ miles) away, where there are several more hotels, holiday apartment blocks and bungalow areas. The Rocamar and Galomar hotels both have rock pools that are open to the general public. To the east is the small stony beach of Reis Magos, which until recently only had a few fishermen's huts on it, used by the locals at weekends. Now it has a hotel, too.

*Enjoying the sea, Caniço de Baixa*

Two roads lead from Caniço to Funchal. The upper road goes there directly, and the low road passes through **Garajau**, which not only has holiday homes and a hotel to offer, but also a fantastic observation point. To reach it, turn off the main road in the direction of Ponta do Garajau. A large statue of Jesus can be seen, and the view from the terrace looks out to Funchal Bay in the west and Ponta da Oliveira in the east.

On a small rise outside Funchal is **Palheiro Golf**, the island's most modern golf course, opened in 1993. It can be reached via the main road from the airport to Funchal. The clubhouse bar, with its wicker furniture, is a good place (even for non-golfers) to lean back over a long drink and indulge in the superb view of Funchal Bay.

# Route 4

## Funchal – Pico do Arieiro – Santana – São Jorge – São Vicente – Porto Moniz – Ribeira Brava – Câmara de Lobos (212km/131 miles)

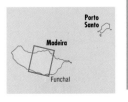

This route leads you around Madeira's highest peaks, first crossing the Poiso Pass to the Pico do Arieiro, the third-highest mountain in Madeira 1,818m (5,964ft). It's actually possible to drive all the way to the summit, and in good weather the panorama is unbelievable. The route continues through dense laurel forests into the fertile and culturally interesting region around Faial, then it's back into the peak district again for a hike up to the Pico Ruivo, the highest mountain on the island (1,862m/6,108ft). The little village of Santana on the north coast with its thatched farmhouses makes a worthwhile stop before journeying on to the picturesque village of São Vicente, where the

*Thatched farmhouse in Santana*

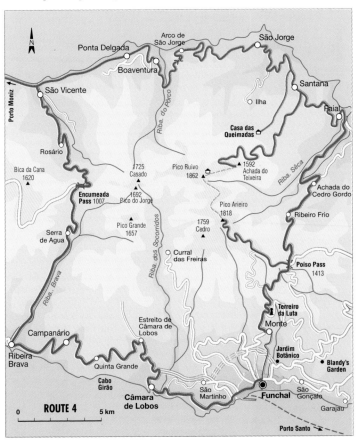

ROUTE 4

*The chapel, Terreiro da Luta*

most impressive section of the coastal route begins. Porto Moniz, with its natural rock pool, is a good place for a swim. The route then continues over the Encumeada Pass to the southern side of the island again to the lively fishing village of Câmara de Lobos. This trip can be done in a day by car or taxi, but allow the possibility of an overnight stay in Santana, São Vicente or Porto Moniz. Those without a car can take a cab to the Pico do Arieiro, hike from there to Santana and then travel the remainder of the route by bus.

Leave Funchal via Monte (*see page 35*) in the direction of the mountains. Soon after the church towers of Monte, the road leads through a dense forest of acacia trees, which in the spring are covered in yellow blossom. From now on there is little human habitation and this region is often shrouded in thick mist as it is within the cloud layer. **Terreiro da Luta**, 7km (4¼ miles), lies roughly 300m (1,000ft) above Monte in the middle of the forest. It can be reached by taking a brief detour along the road to Camacha. At the junction is the former mountain station of the old funicular railway, built in 1912, which used to connect Monte and Terreiro da Luta. The old station is closed, but the small park around it is open to the public and affords an excellent view of Funchal Bay below. A little further on is the **Monument to Our Lady of Peace**, with a flight of steps leading up to it from the road. This is usually a lonely and remote spot; just a few drops of candlewax and dried petals remind visitors of its importance to pilgrims. The statue of the Madonna is perched atop a pedestal made of innumerable tiny sections of basalt. Right next to it is a tiny chapel with a red door and the word *Pax* (peace) on its facade. During World War I, at the behest of Great Britain, Portugal confiscated the property of

*Monument to Our Lady of Peace*

all German inhabitants of the island. Germany then declared war on Portugal in 1916. Madeira was only briefly involved in the hostilities, but one day a German submarine surfaced off Funchal harbour and sank a French battleship anchored there. The terrified locals marched up to Monte in a long procession to pray to the Virgin for peace. During the Mass, the priest vowed to build a monument to the Madonna when the war was over. It was finally completed in 1927; the rusty anchor chain was actually taken from the sunken battleship. A few years ago, many believers were shocked to discover that the statue, whose gaze had always been firmly fixed in the direction of Funchal, was starting to look eastwards. The reason for this is a crack in the monument, roughly at knee height. Since then, more pilgrims than ever have been coming up here to pray, fearing that Our Lady of Peace may be losing her interest in protecting Funchal.

*Madeira cedars*

Higher up into the mountains, enormous Madeira cedars span the road majestically. The famous cathedral roof in Funchal was made from the wood of this gigantic tree, which has become quite rare. At the Poiso Pass, the road branches off towards the ★★ **Pico do Arieiro**, 20km (12 miles), and now winds its way extremely quickly up to the summit. The landscape alters dramatically now to a bare scenario almost resembling moorland, and shaggy-looking sheep quite often tend to jump across the road unexpectedly. The views are truly spectacular from up here: just before the summit there's even a brief glimpse of Funchal far below. For vistas across the north of the island, turn right when the road forks and follow the sign to the **Mirador do Juncal**, accessible via a well-surfaced footpath (the 366-m/400-yd long walk is more than worth it) which provides incredible views of the valleys of Ribeiro Frio and Faja da Nogueira, with their dark-green forests extending away to the coast.

**53**

*The view from Pico do Arieiro*

The large white hotel at the top, the state-owned **Pousada do Pico do Arieiro** was built at the end of the 1980s, and is an ideal starting point for extended hiking trips across the island. In the hotel bar, tired hikers should try a *Poncha,* the house speciality. This fiery drink, composed of sugar-cane spirit, honey and lemon juice, will lend new strength to the limbs, whatever the weather. From the car park, with its souvenir stands run by gentlemen wearing thick pullovers and typically Madeiran woollen hats, it's just a few steps to the summit.

Those keen on hiking further can wander as far as they like from here along the central mountain ridge along a well-surfaced footpath – perhaps the finest route on the island. Pico Ruivo (*see page 55* Santana) is about a 2-hour walk away. This hiking route, which passes the second

*Sea of cloud near Pico Ruivo*

highest peak, Pico das Torres (1,851m/6,073ft) has many superb views of Madeira's bizarre mountain scenery. Remember that good footwear is essential – and a head for heights is also useful!

From the Poiso Pass the route descends into the northern side of the island, so different from the south. The slopes are covered with thick forest dotted with picnic sites, popular with families at weekends. The jungle-like expanse of laurel forest is intersected by only a few footpaths. Near **Ribeiro Frio**, 33km (20 miles), there's a rare chance to learn a little more about this type of forest: a small nature trail has been laid out by the forestry commission, providing information on the most important plants in the laurel forest. The state trout hatchery opposite is also fascinating. Afterwards, Victor's Bar with its open fire is a good place to relax. Anyone here at lunchtime should definitely try the trout – it's guaranteed fresh.

There are several really good walks in the region of Ribeiro Frio. One particularly good detour (roughly 1 hour there and back) leads a short distance below the inns of Ribeiro Frio and then left along the Levada do Furado as far as the Balcões observation point. The view from here extends across a large expanse of the central mountain region, with the highest peaks on Madeira. There's also a longer hike along the Levada do Furado in the opposite direction. A section of dense laurel forest leads to the Lamaceiros water-house; from here it's possible to descend as far as the Portela Pass (the complete hike takes about three hours). This route doesn't have any really taxing ups and downs, but good shoes and a head for heights are essential all the same.

The route leaves the forest area and emerges into an inhabited region once again. Innumerable small terraces (*poios*) line the road, and gorse and daisies bloom at the roadside during spring. At this stage a choice has to be made between two roads, both leading to Faial. The right-hand road is more direct: it seems to head straight for a massive section of mountain towering above the deep valleys. This is the famous Eagle Rock (*Penha de Aguia*), the symbol of northern Madeira (*see also page 46*).

The landscape here is a lot more varied than that of the south. Bananas are rare and only grown on small plots because they are sensitive to the harsher climate, but all kinds of tropical fruits are grown: Japanese medlars, papayas, mangoes and passion fruit. Sugar cane – a real rarity these days – can even be spotted here and there. The small huts between the fields are cattle pens, known as *palheiros*. If you happen to see people (usually women) carrying enormous bundles of grass on their heads, they

*Accommodation for cows*

have usually just cut it to feed their cows or goats and are carrying it back to the pens, where the animals are usually kept.

The first village on the north coast is **Faial**, 43km (26 miles), high above the sea and picturesque with its pretty little church. Just above Faial on a bend is an observation point (*miradouro* ) that mustn't be missed. Follow the coast in the direction of ★★ **Santana**, (pop. 5,000) 53km (32 miles). Just at the entrance to the town there's a small turn-off to the left leading up to **Achada do Teixeira** (1,592m/5,223ft); from there it's just another 45 minutes on foot to the ★ **Pico Ruivo**, along a well-surfaced path. On the way, there is a mountain spring with clear water for drinking. Below the peak is the white Pico Ruivo Inn, where the weary can end the journey. For those still eager to reach the top, the climb up there takes another 15 minutes, but the grandiose panoramic view is well worth the extra trouble.

*Fetching wood in Faial*

Santana is a small town with numerous thatched houses (there are more than a hundred in all). The best place from which to appreciate them properly is the *miradouro* just above the town; nearby, there are two attractive houses that were recently renovated by their owners. Most of the thatched houses are still inhabited; some have been converted into stables for cows. The main road leads past the O Colmo restaurant; the two thatched houses next to it are open to the public. A lot of tourist buses stop here, but the inhabited houses that can be inspected on foot down in the village are actually more authentic and prettier than these rather artificial ones. From here it's not far to Santana's old town hall; the tourist authority has rescued several thatched houses nearby that threatened to become dilapidated.

**55**

Santana has a surprising amount of room. The north coast of Madeira is generally very steep, but here it forms a sort of plateau above the sea, and the *poios* (terraces) are broader than they are elsewhere. A lot of vegetables are grown here, and also the small white willows, the osiers of which are used as raw material by the wickerworkers of Camacha (*see pages 44–5*). This region is especially pretty in spring, when the white flowers of the calla lily bloom at the roadside. Another plant that blossoms around this time is the blueweed and its blue flowers are a common sight on Madeira.

*Waterfall near São Jorge*

On the road to São Jorge, not far from the centre of Santana, is a turn-off to **Queimadas**, 78km (48 miles). This hamlet is reached via a tiny paved road. Thatched holiday houses owned by the state, somewhat larger than their counterparts in Santana and reserved for government officials, stand at the centre of an idyllic park. A detour here

*Vernacular style, São Jorge*

is worthwhile, particularly in spring when the azaleas and the enormous rhododendrons are in bloom. In summer, it's the turn of the native plants, and a profusion of yellow, violet, pink and white greets the visitor.

Santana and the neighbouring community of São Jorge are divided by a deep ravine, the valley of the Ribeira de Sao Jorge, which the road crosses with a lot of difficulty and many hairpin bends. The village of **São Jorge**, 92km (57 miles), lies high above the valley on a mountain ridge. Here, as in Santana, there are several little thatched houses dotted across the fields. The small chapel, with three palm-trees towering above it, is particularly charming. São Jorge is one of the communities on Madeira that has remained most successfully intact. The parks in the centre are full of Bird of Paradise flowers and azaleas.

Close to the chapel is the ★ **parish church of São Jorge**, considered to be one of the most important structures in the northern part of the island. The date above the church portal reads 1761. Not only the main altar but also the side ones are artistically carved and ornately decorated with gold leaf. The chancel is especially magnificent – something quite unexpected in such a tiny village. Only the cathedral in Funchal can compete with the sheer amount of decoration here. At the main altar there is a small statue of St George, and various other reliefs and frescoes depict scenes from the saint's life. Unfortunately, the gold leaf is flaking off, and the interior as a whole is in severe need of restoration.

Not far from the church, in a side street beyond some tall trees, is the *quinta* that once belonged to the landowner, scientist and diplomat Dr João Francisco de Oliveira, who spent many years at the various courts of Europe during the last century.

*São Jorge parish church: details*

The road continues along the north coast now, passing through the little village of **Arco de São Jorge**. Just before the actual houses begin, the As Cabanas restaurant comes into view, high up on the steep coast; there's a souvenir shop here, where all the tourist buses stop during their island round trips. Nevertheless, the ★★ view from the nearby *miradouro* is breathtaking. The houses of Arco de São Jorge lie far below, and the road reaches them after several more hairpins. Today this region has quite a few vineyards; once vegetables were grown, but the hard labour out in the fields is no longer worth it, and many people have moved elsewhere in search of work.

*Ideal conditions for grapes*

A tunnel connects Arco de São Jorge with **Boaventura**, 108km (67 miles). There's not much to see in the village itself, but the Solar de Boaventura, an old mansion hotel, is an ideal place for a restful holiday. It has a gorgeous garden, complete with old-fashioned furniture and camellia blossom.

Further along the coast is the town of **Ponta Delgada**, with its sea-water swimming pool that gets replenished by the surf at every high tide. Once a year, on the first Sunday in September, Ponta Delgada is the main focal point for pilgrims on Madeira. Legend has it that a wooden statue of Christ was washed ashore here during the 15th century, and a chapel was promptly built on the site. The festival here in honour of the *Bom Jesus* has grown increasingly significant over the centuries. The old church was almost completely destroyed by fire in 1908, but a small charred section of the crucifix was successfully rescued. This is worshipped just as fervently as the original cross in the newly built church here.

*Ponta Delgada: church interior*

**57**

One of the most attractive towns on Madeira is ★★ **São Vicente** (pop. 6,500), 117km (72 miles). Its picturesque streets, spruce little houses and many boutiques make an ideal place for a stroll. At the edge of the town, just off the main road, the World Wide Fund for Nature has set up a park containing a collection of all the coastal plants endemic to Madeira. The best time of the year to visit is spring, when the blossom is at its most magnificent. Varieties include the Madeira geranium, blueweed, oxeye daisy and many others.

*Fiesta time at São Vicente*

The **parish church** at the centre of the town, situated next to the steep slope of the São Vicente Valley and surrounded by tall palm trees, is most striking; the small octagonal pavilion next to it is used as a bandstand during festivals. Don't miss a visit to the cemetery: nowhere else on Madeira is the contrast between rich and poor (still a feature of the island today) so obviously displayed. The vaults and tombs of the city's wealthy can be seen among

*Azulejos in the parish church*

*Bunting in the streets, São Vicente*

Bird of Paradise flowers and blueweed, and beside them are the dilapidated graves of the poor.

The imaginative black-and-white mosaic above the church door dates from 1943, the year in which the building was restored. The church was originally built in the 17th century, and is one of the most ornate on the island. The chancel and the side altars are richly decorated with *talha dourada*, the woodcarving style typical of Portuguese churches, covering the entire wall from top to bottom and employing much gold leaf. São Vicente has never been a rich parish and there was not enough gold to cover all the altars, so blue-and-white *azulejos* tiles were used, too. St Vincent can be seen at the main altar, with a picture of a sailing ship beneath him. He appears again on the ceiling of the nave, blessing the town. Although rather naively done, this painting is interesting because it shows what São Vicente looked like long ago when the church was surrounded by just a handful of houses. The panels in the side altars are also striking; they depict the stations of the Cross and were donated to the church by the island's wealthy families. The colourful blue-and-white *azulejos* tiled frieze that runs around the building, so typical of Portuguese churches, is also rather special here because it features not only patterns but actual pictures.

Opposite the church there is a delightful side street that leads a little way uphill and the street that has recently been turned into a pedestrian precinct which runs down towards the main road also has several attractive corners. The inner courtyards, full of flowers, can sometimes be glimpsed along here through open doors.

A detour to the extreme northwestern part of Madeira may be too much for those prone to nervousness. The road along the incredibly steep coastal cliffs was originally cut away with pickaxes, long before the advent of machines. Since then it has been widened and improved, but it's still very adventurous with its narrow passing-places, hairpins, ravines, damp tunnels and above all its free 'car-wash': a waterfall that pours down on to the road unhindered. This wild section of coast ends at ★ **Porto Moniz** (pop. 3,500), 135km (83 miles), a town that lives off its rock pools; their crystal-clear water goes sky blue in good weather. The rocks surrounding the pools and protecting them from the powerful surf are full of all kinds of aquatic life; one or two big waves sometimes splash over into the pools, so the water is regularly replenished. The whole pool area is situated on a single tongue of lava that poured into the sea thousands of years ago, and is now gradually being eroded by the ocean. Porto Moniz is also a wine town, and is enjoying a boom in tourism at present. The restaurants are full of day-trippers, and in summer the boarding houses, holiday homes and camp site are popular not just with tourists from abroad but Madeirans too.

Leave the north coast at São Vicente and travel southwards along the valley of the same name. After heavy rain, the forested slopes to the right become awash with waterfalls. Soon, on the left-hand side of the road, the Rosario bell tower will come into view. This unusual-looking structure is actually a chapel, consisting of just one tower. Built in the middle of this century, it dominates the valley above São Vicente. The mountains here are often heavy with cloud, and the landscape as a whole is reminiscent of a tropical rain forest. It's quite a shock to suddenly break through the cloud layer and arrive at the **Encumeada Pass**, 164km (101 miles), which is actually the island's lowest mountain pass (1,007m/3,303ft). From the large observation point at the top of the pass in good weather there's a simultaneous view of the north and south coasts, although the north coast is usually obscured by cloud.

*Heading for the Encumeada Pass*

The route leads southwards along the terraced slopes of the Ribeira Brava valley. On the right-hand side is the Pousada dos Vinháticos, another state-run mountain hotel, with a view that can be enjoyed over a coffee on the terrace, or another option is to follow the narrow path across to the nearby *miradouro*. The road travels down to the bottom of the valley, poplar trees and giant reeds can be seen everywhere, and it's down here in wintertime that the Ribeira Brava ('wild river') lives up to its name as it pours across the enormous blocks of basalt.

The weather in the town of ★ **Ribeira Brava** (pop. 9,000), 178km (110 miles) is almost always pleasant. The town has a distinctive atmosphere of its own, and the cafés on the promenade have sunny terraces with views of the sea. Nearby there are several good shops and also a small market hall, selling fresh produce that ranges from fruit and vegetables to massive tuna fish. The town's old cobbled main street, the Rua do Visconde, leads straight through the centre. On the right, hidden behind trees in a small park, there is a magnificent old mansion, painted pink, with white window frames and green shutters. Today this building, which dates from 1776, is the **Town Hall** of Ribeira Brava. The grounds are open to the public and many of the large old trees here bear their botanical names.

*Promenade café, Ribeira Brava*

Directly opposite is the **parish church of São Bento**; it's hard to spot from the main road, and the entrance is on the other side. The enormous square outside the church is decorated black-and-white, and the building's baroque facade appears rather stern. This is offset by the *azulejos* blue-and-white tiles on the belfry. A painting next to the portal commemorates a great event in Ribeira Brava's history that took place on 8 April 1848 when the statue

*The belfry of São Bento*

*The interior of the church*

of Our Lady of Fátima stopped by here on a visit during its world tour. The church underwent extensive renovation during the baroque period (the magnificent altars date from that time), but a further and rather disappointing restoration took place more recently. Several sections remain of the original structure, which is one of the oldest on the whole island: the first church on the site was built in around 1440. The highlight inside is the Manueline font, which can be admired inside its very own chapel, just to the right of the main entrance: mysterious mythological creatures have been carved into the stone, along with floral motifs and some barely decipherable lettering. The pulpit is also a valuable example of stonework decoration dating from the reign of King Manuel.

On the road to Funchal just above the town there is a brief turn-off to the right leading to a *miradouro* which has a view back across Ribeira Brava and as far as the west coast and Ponta do Sol. From now on the road starts to wind above the south coast through a densely populated area. Bananas are grown around here, along with several other kinds of fruit and vegetable. Between all the fields are the unmistakeably Madeiran whitewashed houses, with their bright-red tiled roofs.

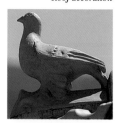

*Roof decoration*

The next stop is the observation point known as ★ **Cabo Girão**, 192km (119 miles). The sign here says 580m (1,900ft) – and that's the distance downwards vertically to the narrow strip of coastline and dark pebble beach far, far below. Amazingly, there are even a few *poios* (terraces) along the steep mountain wall; access to them must be extremely difficult. There's also a view across to Funchal on the left, with the limeworks at Câmara de Lobos in the foreground.

*Ribeira Brava*

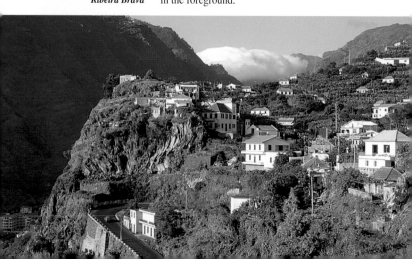

Vineyards are typical of the scenery near **Estreito de Câmara de Lobos**. The town itself is rather quiet, apart from its extremely busy weekend market. Every Sunday the market hall is jammed to bursting when all the farmers of the region arrive with their cows, goats and sheep – all of them for sale, along with the fruit and vegetables and everything else. Estreito de Câmara de Lobos also comes to life in September during the wine harvest. A firm in the town turns the grapes into Madeira wine (*see page 82*). The high point of harvest time is the wine festival; visitors can not only eat and drink to their heart's content, but can also be introduced to the ancient art of treading grapes.

Below Estreito, right next to the sea, is the little fishing town of ★ **Câmara de Lobos**, 204km (126 miles). The main attraction here is the harbour, which is one of the most important on Madeira. Several of the colourfully painted open wooden boats can be seen lying at anchor in the protected bay; others have been pulled up the beach. The fishermen can be seen calmly and methodically mending the long lines they use to catch the *espada*, or cutlass fish (*see page 81*); others sit around playing cards. The men only sail out of the harbour three times a week on average as the Atlantic is far too stormy for small craft. Sometimes it's possible to observe a new wooden boat being built at the nearby shipyard. Don't miss a quick look inside the fishermen's chapel of **Nossa Senhora da Conceição** at the harbour, which was built in 1420 and renovated during the 18th century. The walls are decorated with oil paintings depicting scenes from the life of St Pedro Goncalves Telmo, the patron saint of Portuguese sailors. The gilt baroque altar with its statue of the Virgin is most ornate; the motif is repeated on the building's colourfully painted wooden roof.

The people of Câmara de Lobos are very poor – the fishing doesn't bring in a lot of money. This is why the narrow streets of the town are full of women embroidering, trying to eke out a meagre family income, and the children are dressed only in the bare essentials; this sight, though picturesque for visitors, reflects bitter social realities.

The pavement mosaic in front of the parish church of São Sebastião bears the date of its foundation – 1430. However, during the baroque period the church was completely rebuilt. On the ceiling is a painting of St Sebastian, patron saint of the town. The rather elegant combination of gilt and white paint on the altars contrasts with the rather uneven *azulejos* tile decoration on the walls.

The bandstand in the square outside the church is used during all the festivals here, and an arbour separates the square from the sea. Sit down on one of the benches in the shade of the palm trees and admire the view of nearby Cabo Girão.

*Pruning palms, Câmara de Lobos*

*The protected bay*

*Traditional boat building*

*Poverty on the streets*

*Crossing the Encumeada Pass*

*Hiking the levadas*

# Route 5

## Ribeira Brava – Paúl da Serra – Rabaçal – Ponta do Pargo – Paúl do Mar – Calheta – Ponta do Sol (165km/102 miles)

This route reveals the delights of western Madeira. It follows the coast road from Funchal to Ribeira Brava, then turns inland towards the Encumeada Pass, marking the start of an attractive stretch across to the bare and windswept plateau of Paúl da Serra. A detour to Rabaçal is worthwhile at this point; it's a good base for walks or extended hikes through almost untouched jungle landscape, along Madeira's famed *levadas* (*see page 9*). The route then continues across the plateau, which grows increasingly narrow as it descends towards the coast. A less-travelled route leads to Ponta do Pargo, Madeira's westernmost point, with its lighthouse. The journey then continues through fertile landscape as far as Calheta, the main town in the southwestern part of the island, and from there via Ribeira Brava and back to Funchal.

The trip can be interrupted along the way at all sorts of interesting places, to admire village churches and chapels and to explore the various coastal towns, many of them still largely untouched by tourism. The whole trip takes a day by car or taxi, but an overnight stay in Porto Moniz or Prazeres may also be a good idea. The towns and villages along the southwest and west coasts can be reached by bus, but not the Paúl da Serra plateau.

Leave Funchal on the main road signposted to Câmara de Lobos, and then take the winding road to Ribeira Brava, 27km (16 miles). Here the road branches off towards the centre of the island and the Encumeada Pass. At the top of the pass there's a small bar – a good place for a hot coffee before embarking on the remote stretch of road signposted to the mountain Bica da Cana. There's scarcely any human habitation, let alone a restaurant, for miles around here. By the way, watch out for falling rocks! These tend to tumble down the slopes after heavy rain, which is why the Madeirans prefer to use the left-hand lane whenever there's no traffic coming the other way. But don't let that put you off travelling along this truly panoramic route. There are all kinds of fantastic views of the south coast along here; up on the right are enormous vertical basalt pillars, and water can be seen pouring down from the rocks. It's worthwhile making a short stop at the Lombo do Mouro, to enjoy the breathtaking view.

*Paúl da Serra plateau*

The ★ **Paúl da Serra plateau** now begins. In winter, when the dried bracken covers the ground, this region tends to be rather dreary and forlorn-looking. In summer the grass grows again, providing pastureland for the numerous sheep. A few houses and some trees come into view on the right, and soon the observation point known as the **Bica da Cana**, 46km (28 miles) appears. The last few yards to this *miradouro* need to be covered on foot;

63

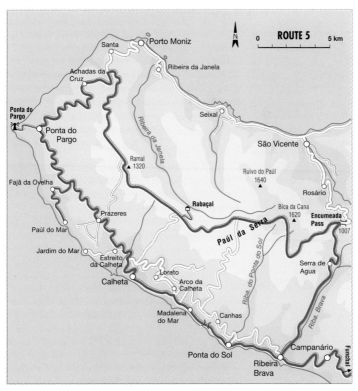

*Risco Falls, Rabaçal*

*Enchanted forest*

just follow the paved path from the forest lodge. Finally there's a view, 1,620m (5,315ft) up, right down into the valley of São Vicente and beyond the Encumeada Pass across to the highest peaks of Madeira.

In foggy conditions – all too frequent up here – the plateau is reminiscent of the moors in the Scottish Highlands. When the sun comes out, the Paúl da Serra (the name means 'mountain moor') suddenly appears quite cheerful. Gradually, almost imperceptibly, the road begins to descend as the plateau gradually becomes narrower, and soon the coast can be seen on both sides. Even in foggy conditions, the cloud will part from time to time, providing views of the tiny houses with their red-tiled roofs dotting the landscape in the south.

On the right the road turns off to **Rabaçal**, 54km (33 miles) down a hairy, narrow lane through thick green laurel jungle. Passing places are rare and motorists are advised to exercise special caution! This road is actually a dead end, leading to Rabaçal, which is just a small holiday village especially reserved for Portuguese government employees. The area around Rabaçal is criss-crossed with a network of *levadas* (*see page 9*) which make good hiking trails: popular destinations include the ★ **Risco Falls**, two narrow and seemingly endless cascades. The broad path that leads there begins at the car park, where it descends and then carries straight along the (rather aptly named) *Levada do Risco* (the walk there and back takes 45 minutes). A less demanding and perhaps even more attractive hiking destination are the ★ **25 Springs** (two hours there and back). The walk from the *Levada do Risco* down to the *Levada dos 25 Fontes* leads through a delightful, seemingly enchanted stretch of forest, full of enormous trees festooned with lichen; the *levada* then leads off to the right to the bubbling springs.

The landscape on the plateau is yellow in spring, when the gorse is in bloom. The bushes are round in shape and resemble large cushions – they are regularly nibbled at by sheep and goats.

The route leads steeply down the northern slope of the island, where the vegetation starts getting more varied. At first the road is lined with heather – not the type common in Europe, but a much larger, more bushy variety – and then the laurel forest suddenly begins. At this stage the road forks: take the left turn signposted to Funchal. One of the most remote regions of Madeira now lies ahead. It's rare to see any tourists here; only a few cars use this stretch. The region is particularly pretty in summer, when hydrangeas and agapanthus grow by the roadside. Pass the lonely looking A Carreta restaurant (it's one of the only places in western Madeira that offers lunch) and the hamlet of Ribeira da Vaca comes into view.

Near **Ponta do Pargo**, 92km (57 miles), the landscape starts broadening out. The coastal region of Madeira is rarely as flat as it is here; indeed, there's so much room that the local farmers can actually use machinery. The small brown cows are native to the island. Look out for the signpost to **Farol**, the westernmost point of Madeira. The red tip of the lighthouse is soon visible, high above the steep coast. A lighthouse keeper still lives in it, even though the light has been operating automatically for several years. The view westwards across the endless expanse of ocean is quite awe-inspiring – there's no land at all between here and America.

*The lighthouse*

A tiny road leads down steeply towards ★ **Paúl do Mar**, 109km (67 miles). The village has an enormous araucaria at its centre, and the houses stand among the banana plantations along the small coastal strip. The middle of the village with its narrow streets and houses all huddled together is completely dwarfed by the dark and massive wall of rock directly above it. Paúl do Mar is one of the few villages on Madeira that was built directly next to the sea. The waves crash against the solidly built harbour promenade, and from the narrow quay beside the stony beach there's a good view of the nearby beauty spot **Jardim do Mar**, although there's no road connection to it from here. The small shrine to Santo Amaro looks as if it were built by the villagers to ward off the evil influence of the sea. The fishing boats, green and blue, lie high above the sea; they can only be taken out in calm weather, and travel down a slip whenever necessary.

*Paúl do Mar: the shrine*

**65**

Women can often be seen washing their laundry in a small waterfall nearby. There's even a little market hall, where the local fishermen's meagre catches are auctioned off. The chimneys of two old sugar mills can also be seen; sugar cane was still being grown here a few decades ago.

*Soaking up the sun*

*Messing around in boats*

The gulf between rich and poor on Madeira is particularly striking here in Paúl do Mar, too. A lot of large houses have been built on the edge of the village by returned emigrés in recent years. They left the village originally to make their fortunes overseas. Many come back once they've retired and begin a new existence in their homeland with the money earned. The construction of the village's modern church was financed by emigrés. There are two small restaurants in Paúl do Mar; another one, which rather resembles a flying saucer, hovers high above the steep coast on the road that leads back via Fajã da Ovelha to the main road.

The only human habitation around here is along the mountain ridges. Deep ravines separate the villages. Above the agricultural land the road runs through tranquil pine forests, above and below the *levada* that brings irrigation water down from the Paúl da Serra plateau. A new hotel called the Jardim Atlantico has been opened in **Prazeres**, 122km (75 miles) and makes a good base for a walking tour to Paúl do Mar along one of the old, paved connecting routes that once covered the island. It has a superb view that extends as far as Paúl do Mar and Jardim do Mar. The region around Prazeres still contains many old one-room houses built from dark basalt and which have unplastered walls. The village church with its massive towers appears far too large for the place.

Near **Estreito da Calheta**, 126 km (78 miles), the landscape broadens out, providing a great view across the mountain range to the east, dotted with numerous tiny red-roofed houses. The main sight in the village is the ★ **Chapel of the Three Magi** (*Capela dos Reis Magos*), which dates from the 16th century, found down a small side road just after the turn-off to Jardim do Mar. The

*Hotel in Prazeres*

whitewashed building is a simple affair, with a tiny belfry and the crucifix symbol of the Order of the Cross up on its gable. Carved in stone above the simple entrance is the coat of arms of the founder, Francisco de Gouveia, a rich landowner from Estreito da Calheta. The chapel is always kept locked, but the key may be obtained from the house next door on request. The altarpiece inside is reputed to be 460 years old; the valuable carving at its centre depicts the Three Magi. The altar wings are decorated with Flemish panel paintings containing scenes from the lives of saints. The unpretentious, Mudejar-style wooden ceiling is very attractive, as are the Manueline carvings on the small side-windows.

The town of **Calheta** (pop. 5,500), 131km (81 miles), could be termed the capital of southwestern Madeira. A new apartment building with shops has been built in the upper section of the town, and looks a bit out of place. No one is all that keen to move into these apartments, since most people in Calheta have houses of their own. Drive down towards the sea along a small ravine and the real centre of the village, with the ★ **parish church**, comes into view. The church is usually closed but it's worth asking next door for the key. A good opportunity to go inside is just before daily Mass; the times are posted on the main door. The elegant stonework on the main portal dates from the Manueline era. Work began on this church in around 1430, but the building has undergone several alterations since then. The chapel in the side aisle contains the church's most valuable treasure, the Most Holy Sacrament, made out of silver and ebony. The wooden Mudejar-style ceiling in the choir is also worthy of note.

*Calheta parish church*

Right next to the church is one of the three sugar mills on Madeira that still produce rum and molasses. The chimneys of several disused sugar mills can still be seen along the coastal strip near Calheta – mute reminders of the time when sugar cane was an important crop. The beach at Calheta is stony, but a concrete platform has been built with changing cabins and toilet facilities; a ramp allows easy access to the sea. The terrace of the Onda Azul restaurant is a good place to soak up the sunshine, sip at a long drink and gaze out to sea. Nearby is a brand-new docking area, with several open fishing boats. The Funchal-Calheta excursion ship docks at the quay.

The tiny centre of **Madalena do Mar**, 134km (83 miles), contains an attractively restored **church**. The original 15th-century structure was almost completely renewed during the baroque period, and the interior decoration – including the valuable gilt altars, painted coffered ceiling and colourful pulpit – dates from that time. An avenue of palm trees leads across the long courtyard outside the church to its front portal.

*Madalena do Mar*

*Ponta do Sol*

The houses of Madalena do Mar extend a long way along the coast. A new road now separates them from the ocean, which until a few years ago was almost right outside their front doors. Now there's a sea wall to protect the houses and the rest of the village from the waves.

The road enters a long tunnel, damp and dripping, before continuing along the base of the steep coast as far as **Ponta do Sol**, 138km (85 miles). It is worth stopping here if only for the colourful **kiosk** on the harbour promenade, where visitors can enjoy a cup of coffee and appreciate the amazingly ornate furniture. A cobbled street leads to the churchyard and the parish church of ★ **Nossa Senhora da Luz**. Enter it through the rather stern-looking baroque portal. Immediately on the right is a green ceramic font; it was a personal gift from King Manuel I to the church of Ponta do Sol. The restored coffered ceiling depicts scenes from the life of the Virgin. The tiled frieze in the nave has also been renewed; it contains some yellow alongside the traditional *azulejos* blue-and-white. The real highlight of this church is the carved Mudejar-style wooden ceiling of the chancel, which probably dates from 1500. The paintings on it are not so old.

*The kiosk on the promenade*

Fans of American literature should take a few steps up the hill behind the church. Across the stream on the left is an old town house which is now the town hall. The ancestors of the famous American novelist John Dos Passos (1896–1970) lived here.

Above the church is the Parque Infante Dom Henrique, a pleasant little cobbled square shaded by palm trees. From the observation terrace there's a view of the stony beach, and of the small docks of Ponta do Sol that have been cleverly integrated into a natural rock barrier. Slightly above the square there is also an attractive little baroque chapel.

# Route 6

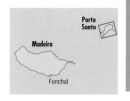

## ★★ Porto Santo – the beach island

Porto Santo is worth a trip in its own right, if not for an entire holiday – but only for those in search of peace and relaxation, because Madeira's little neighbouring island is actually rather a sleepy place. Its 5,000 or so inhabitants live in comparatively flat, desert-like countryside on an island measuring 13km (8 miles) by 6km (4 miles). Porto Santo has little agriculture to speak of: there are a few vineyards, and melons are sold to Madeira.

*On the edge of Europe*

The airport runway, far longer than the one on Madeira, cuts the island into two sections. However, there's hardly any air traffic at all here apart from a few daily flights made to and from Madeira by a small turboprop plane; the odd larger plane also arrives now and then on its way to Lisbon. The handful of soldiers stationed near the airport provides the population with food and work. There's tourism too, of course, but it's still in its infancy.

*The beach is almost empty*

The island's real highlight is its wonderful white sandy beach, unique in the archipelago, 8km (5 miles) long and hardly built up at all. It gets a bit crowded during the summer when Madeiran families come over for their holidays, but for the rest of the year it's more or less empty – and Porto Santo is usually sunny. The crossing by ferry boat from Madeira takes 90 minutes, and can often be rather bumpy. Don't be alarmed at having to go through it all again on the return journey: the trip is usually smoother the other way as the boat seems to travel effortlessly over the waves, which usually flow from the northeast. The rather more expensive alternative to the ferry is a 15-minute trip by propeller plane.

## History

The Portuguese claimed Porto Santo in 1418, several months before Madeira. Bartolomeu Perestrelo, who was later to become Christopher Columbus' father-in-law, became the first governor of Porto Santo and laid out a settlement on the island. The first inhabitants found fertile land, burned away the existing vegetation and then planted cereal. The sailing ships that plied the Atlantic during that time used to stock up on foodstuffs here – something hard to imagine today. The deforestation was not without its consequences: the island dried up, and rain gradually washed the fertile soil into the sea.

Porto Santo – difficult to defend or fortify – was also a popular target for pirates. North African corsairs not only ransacked the island regularly but also enslaved many inhabitants, and the island had become almost completely abandoned by the time its agriculture was given a new

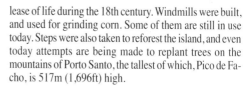

*Vila Baleira*

**70**

*Model of Columbus' caravel*

lease of life during the 18th century. Windmills were built, and used for grinding corn. Some of them are still in use today. Steps were also taken to reforest the island, and even today attempts are being made to replant trees on the mountains of Porto Santo, the tallest of which, Pico de Facho, is 517m (1,696ft) high.

## Island tour

Almost half the population of Porto Santo lives in **Vila Baleira**. With its palm trees and whitewashed houses, the island's capital is an attractive town. A good way to get an initial, general impression of the place is to drink a coffee on the terrace of the Café Baiana, observe the comings and goings of the island's bright yellow taxicabs (all 19 of them) and watch the old men whiling away the time of day in the leafy Town Hall Square (*Largo do Pelourinho*). The **Town Hall**, with its dracena palm outside the entrance, dates from the 16th century. Right next to it is the parish church of **Nossa Senhora da Piedade**, with its blue-and-white *azulejos* medallion under the bright-red tiled roof. It suffered continual damage at the hands of pirates and, although first built only a few years after Porto Santo was discovered, the church underwent a total renovation during the baroque period.

Hidden away in a street behind the church is the ★ **Columbus Museum** containing many exhibits connected with the life of the great seafarer. The house next door to the museum was reputedly lived in by Columbus for several years before his famous Atlantic crossing: it is believed that he lived here with his wife Felipa Moniz, daughter of Porto Santo's first governor. The house looks as if it was built somewhat later, however – probably during the 16th century! A palm-tree-lined avenue leads from the town hall towards the sea and the beach, where there are changing cabins, showers and also several restaurants and shops.

A standard ingredient of any tour of Porto Santo is a drive up to the impressive **Pico do Castelo** (437m/1,433ft), which from a distance is somewhat reminiscent of the 'Sugar Loaf' near Rio. It takes about 20 minutes to walk from the car park at the observation terrace to the castle on the summit, which was once used as a hideaway from the pirates by the inhabitants. It's not essential to go all the way up to the top, because a good view of Vila Baleira and the plain can be enjoyed just as much from the observation terrace.

The route now continues on to **Camacha**, the largest town in the northern part of the island. Next

door to the windmill, on the other side of the former thresh-
ing-floor, stands a typical old house of Porto Santo: it is
built of large stones without any mortar, and covered with
wooden beams and a clay roof. It contains the Estrela do
Norte restaurant; try the grilled chicken here accompanied
by the emerald-coloured local wine (*Verdelho*). A word of
warning: Porto Santo is a sunny place, and the wines here
have an average alcohol content of around 13 percent.

Pass the airport runway now, and cross the vineyards
of Camacha to the bizarre north coast. Here the **Fonte
da Areia** can be seen bubbling beneath massive limestone
formations. An impermeable, subterranean layer of basalt
prevents the water from sinking any further into the ground
here, and this spring is thought to have healing properties;
some even believe it can rejuvenate body and soul.

The main road on the island passes the highest parts,
concentrated in the northeast, and goes through the tiny
farming villages of Serra de Dentro and Serra de Fora
before reaching the south coast again at the **Portela** observation point. This *miradouro*, by the way, is the best
place to get an overall idea of the island's beach.

The beach road to the west of Vila Baleira should certainly be driven along. A detour to Campo de Cima is a
must to see its windmills. In Campo de Baixo, holiday
homes owned by foreigners are springing up like mush-
rooms. In Ponta there's a riding school and ambitious plans
are already afoot to create a golf course here. No buyer has
been found as yet for the not-quite-completed Novo
Mundo hotel, which is growing more dilapidated by the
day. The route now reaches the southwestern point of Porto
Santo, the ★ **Ponta da Calheta**. It's fun exploring the
weird coastal rock formations here, and there's a good
view across to the **Ilheu de Baixo**, a small uninhabited
island just off the coast.

*Windmill at Camacha*

**71**

*The coast at Fonte da Areia*

# Artistic Heritage

## Architecture

The architecture of Madeira has always reflected the deep gulf between rich and poor. The rural population lived in tiny, straw-thatched huts consisting of little more than a single room. Similar houses are thought to have existed in Portugal during the Early Christian period. Many of the huts on Madeira were torn down or turned into cattle pens over the centuries, but in the more remote regions – especially in the north and the southwest – they still exist and several are still inhabited.

During feudal times, there were several manor houses at the centre of the estates they controlled, but few have survived the ravages of time. Their owners were not all that interested in rural life anyway. By the time the sugar industry went into recession (mid-16th century), landowners were already parcelling out their country estates to leaseholders and moving to Funchal. The old mansions (*quintas*) there still testify to the wealth of their former owners. From the outside they often appear rather forbidding, but inside there are splendid inner courtyards with elegant galleries surrounding them.

*Quinta Spléndida*

**73**

King Manuel I ascended the throne in 1495, and an architectural style distinctive of the island is named after him: Manueline. It is characterised by imaginatively playful ornamentation in carved stone, and most of the churches on Madeira date from this period. Although less ornate than many in mainland Portugal, the buildings were decorated with a great deal of imaginative carving, often featuring fabulous creatures from faraway countries, or various seafaring motifs. Carved wooden ceilings were also fashionable at that time; they were created by Moorish artists, and the churches on Madeira contain several excellent examples, ranging from simple to ornate.

*Manueline style, Funchal*

Very little was built during Spanish rule. It was only during the 18th century that architecture on Madeira experienced a new lease of life. The baroque style was in vogue in Europe at that time, and was extravagantly celebrated in Portugal thanks to the large quantities of gold the country was receiving from its South American colony of Brazil. The churches in particular benefited from this: they were filled with magnificent altars carved in wood and decorated with gold leaf (*talha dourada*).

*Talha dourada*

The typically Portuguese craft of tile-making also reached its zenith at this time, and walls, staircases, floors, benches, churches, inside and out, were covered with *azulejos*, or tile-pictures, usually coloured blue and white. The earliest style of tilework has Spanish-Arabian origins – the *Mudejar* style, named after the Muslims who had converted to Christianity – recognised by their strict geometrical pattern. Over the centuries, patterns multiplied and grew into 'tile carpets', the best examples of which can be found in churches. By the end of the 17th century, the first figures and motifs appeared.

## Art

As far as painting is concerned, Madeira has little it can claim as its own, but the island does possess one of the most comprehensive collections of Flemish paintings in the world, dating from the 15th and 16th centuries. Noblemen and wealthy merchants commissioned the paintings from artists in Flanders, paying for them with sugar. Madeira also has a cultural association devoted to contemporary art (Cine Forum de Funchal), and the young Madeiran artists Maria da Paz Nobrega and Carlos Luz have produced some good island landscapes.

*Flemish painting*

## Crafts

There is plenty of original art to be found in Madeira – embroidery and wickerwork, which provide a vital contribution towards the family income, albeit a small one. Mainly it is women from the traditional fishing villages or the villages deserted by emigration who spend their time embroidering. It is still a craft passed on from mothers to daughters, although the young girls have ambitions further afield these days. Madeiran embroidery is famous worldwide; wherever you go on the island, vendors spread out tablecloths, collars, napkins and handkerchiefs all hand-embroidered in eye-catching patterns.

*Embroiderers depicted in tile*

It isn't only embroidery at which the needlewomen of Madeira are skilled. They also excel at tapestry, copying works of art and Madeiran landscapes.

Wickerwork as an art originates from the mid-19th century, although wicker baskets have been made since the building of the first *levadas* when they were used for lowering the workers down the steep cliffs. Today the willow canes are not only woven into countless styles of basket, but animals and other ornamental shapes of all sizes can be skilfully created – some works of art, such as life-size farm animals, take up to six months to make.

*Mona Lisa tapestry*

The Madeiran Institute of Embroidery, Tapestry and Handicrafts was set up in 1978. The museum in Funchal contains exhibits dating back to 1870 and is well worth a visit.

## Sugar-box furniture

In 1508 King Manuel I granted Funchal its coat of arms: five sugar loaves in the shape of a cross. Madeira had grown rich from its exported sugar, and the custom in those days was to allow the sugar to crystallise in cone-shaped clay containers, thus creating the 'sugar loaves'.

*Balmy evening in Funchal*

During the second half of the 16th century, competition from Brazil began to make the Madeiran sugar producers' lives increasingly difficult, and eventually the islanders decided to import sugar from Brazil but then send it on as Madeira sugar. Brazilian sugar arrived in packing-cases made of real mahogany. Discovering this wood pleased the Madeirans greatly, and carpenters soon began to make furniture out of empty Brazilian sugar crates. Cupboards and chests with the strange name of 'sugar-box furniture' were produced throughout the 17th century.

They were simply and solidly built, and are typical of the Portuguese rural furniture of that time; the doors were often coffered and provided with heavy iron locks in the shape of crosses or flowers. The style soon grew to be accepted, and sugar-box furniture was produced from native woods as well. When the English merchants arrived on Madeira at about 1700 they brought an entirely new style with them, and this spelt the end for sugar-box furniture. Today original items of sugar-box furniture are popular with collectors, and many pieces can still be admired in the island's museums and private houses.

### Theatre

The theatre in Funchal has no permanent ensemble, but troupes from the mainland are regular visitors. Classical concerts are also given now and then in the theatre, especially during the Bach Festival which takes place in June. The famous Portuguese *fado*, a type of ballad accompanied by the guitar, is also popular on Madeira. There are *fado* bars, and hotels often have *fado* evenings. The *fado* was created in Portugal as an expression of the grief and pain deep in the Portuguese soul (*saudade*), but it is gradually being usurped by the more cheerful influence of Brazil – a result of the import of popular culture from the former colony.

*Traditional dance*

# Festivals and Folklore

## Traditional dress

*Ideal headgear*

The Portuguese have always had a particular fondness for hats. Each region of the country has its own special shape of hat and several of these variations arrived on Madeira with the Portuguese settlers. In Madeira's rural areas, and especially in the mountains, hand-knitted woollen hats (*Barrete de Lã*) are still a common sight. In wintertime when the mountains are cold, many tourists cannot resist buying one of these warm hats from souvenir stalls. In summer the same hats seem to be worn for one reason alone: without them, a man just isn't properly dressed.

Knee-high leather boots were also part of the traditional dress here until quite recently, but in many places they have now been replaced by wellingtons. Otherwise, folkwear seems to have disappeared from public life. It is still worn by the women who sell flowers in Funchal: colourful woollen dresses, white blouses with a red cloth thrown over the shoulder, and the funny little cap with its bobble. The wicker sled drivers in Monte (*see page 37*) also wear traditional male folk dress: white trousers, a shirt with a cummerbund, and a boater.

## Music and dancing

*Villagers celebrate in costume*

Each village has its own dancing groups, who perform during the year's major festivals such as Christmas and Easter. Professional groups performing in restaurants and hotels introduce spectators to a folklore that is still genuine: some dances date back to the time of Moorish slavery, others were introduced to the islands by immigrants from northern Portugal. Many of the songs date from the hard work in the fields or at the winepresses, others were sung by pilgrims or during church festivals.

## Church festivals

There's a patron saint – sometimes even two or three – for every village on Madeira and many colourful festivals are held in their honour during the summer. Weeks before a great event the streets are already decked with garlands of flowers, and the actual celebrations continue right through Saturday night into Sunday morning. Firework displays are held, and the traditional meat dish known as *espetada* is consumed in great quantities. After the meal the singing and dancing begins, and continues into the small hours. On the Sunday morning the villagers dress in black and carry the statue of the saint around the church in a solemn procession. The religious rite is soon over and the rest of the day is devoted to the family. Solemn-faced fathers, mothers and grandparents, holding their children by the hand, go on afternoon strolls through the streets.

*Putting up the bunting*

Since the exact dates of certain festivals can vary quite a bit, it's best to double-check at tourist information offices for details of festivals.

*Festival time, Curral das Freiras*

**5 January** Santo Amaro at Santa Cruz.

**20 January** S. Sebastião, at Caniçal, Câmara de Lobos.

**February** *Festa dos Compadres* (Godfathers' Festival): held one week before the Carnival in Santana and other places. Shrovetide Carnival takes four days and is celebrated all over the island with the high point being a colourful procession Brazilian style in Funchal.

**April** Flower Festival in Funchal. Parade with flower-festooned floats.

*Flowers in Funchal*

**29 June** Festival of St Peter, the patron saint of fishermen, Ribeira Brava. Boat procession.

**End of June** Sheep-Shearing Festival in Paúl da Serra. A folk festival held while the sheep are being sheared.

**End of July** Folklore Festival '24-hour dance', Santana.

**15 August** Assumption of the Virgin Mary in Monte. Large pilgrimage procession. The most important folk festival on Madeira.

**First Sunday in September** *Festa do Senhor Bom Jesus* in Ponta Delgada.

**8 – 9 September** *Festa do Senhor dos Milagres* Machico. Nocturnal procession honouring the Lord of Miracles.

**Mid-September** Wine Festival. Wine-tasting and exhibitions in Funchal.

*The grape harvest*

**Third weekend in September** *Festa Nossa Senhora da Piedade* in Caniçal. Waterborne procession in celebration of Our Lady of Piety.

**1 November** Chestnut Festival held in Curral das Freiras.

**Christmas** Coloured lights are put up everywhere on 8 December and only removed on 6 January. 25 December is a family holiday.

**New Year's Eve** Famous firework display in Funchal.

# Food and Drink

The Madeirans generally adhere to what might be termed a rather limited diet – mostly Portuguese influenced with a dash of Arabian spice – although they eat far less meat than the mainland.

The cuisine suits every palate. The most popular methods of cooking are *frito* or *grelhado* – roasted or grilled – with plenty of aromatic seasonings. The alluring smells of fennel, garlic, lemon and laurel which float around the Madeiran gardens and countryside in summer also eminate from the cooking pots. Caraway seed is also used in abundance and no cook would dream of leaving out a dash of local wine.

*Add some peppers*

A typical menu begins with a filling vegetable or fish soup; for the main course there is usually fish or meat with side dishes. The vegetables are often boiled for far too long despite the fact that Madeira produces a wide variety, as is clear from a visit to any market hall. Salads usually have to be ordered as an extra, since they qualify as a starter. Pudding is an extravagant affair, as in Portugal. All kinds of different cakes and trifles are available (often extremely sweet), but also fruit salad and ice cream. The different gateaux and desserts can often be chosen from a special buffet trolley.

*The complete meal*

**79**

Tourists often start growing distrustful when they notice an extra charge for bread and butter on the bill, but there's no fraud involved: even in restaurants frequented by locals, it's the done thing to place bread and butter on the table to quell the initial pangs of hunger during the wait for the first course. Diners are usually charged for the bread and butter whether they've touched it or not.

Another tip: don't be amazed in some of the better restaurants if the waiter starts clearing away a lot of the cutlery on the table the moment you've given him your order. If there are too many laid places, they are simply cleared away, along with unnecessary wine glasses, etc. This is simply the done thing on Madeira.

Paying the bill also differs from the European norm: it doesn't matter how many people are seated at the table, the waiter will insist on bringing a single bill for everyone. Trying to break it down into its individual components is almost impossible. Those who wish to pay separately should always say so before they order. Tips are included in the bill, but it's normal to leave a few extra coins on the table for friendly service. Locals usually give around 20 escudos a head; tourists are generally expected to leave a bit more. Don't worry about it falling into the wrong hands: the waiters keep their eyes open.

On the whole, you can still eat well and relatively inexpensively on Madeira.

*Freshly caught fish*

## Specialities

Madeira is well-known for its *espetada*, a gigantic piece of skewered meat that is eaten at folk festivals and most other occasions too. Eating *espetadas* can turn into a real event in some restaurants in the country districts, where the meat is cooked in front of diners over an open fire and then hung on the ceiling above the table. Each guest then takes off as much meat as he can manage, and the procedure continues until all have eaten their fill.

*Oysters*

Those keen on trying an authentically local dish should try ordering goat, which is most commonly available around Easter time. Braised for hours in the oven and accompanied by all sorts of herbs, it tastes absolutely delicious. Seafood should be eaten in the coastal towns, where many restaurants serve it freshly caught. The *espada* (cutlass fish) is an integral part of every menu, and is often served in puff pastry with banana. Tuna is almost as common, although several other kinds of fish are also available depending on the season. They are chosen either from the freezer or from a tray brought by the waiter, and come either grilled or fried. Those keen on shrimp or crayfish should remember that these are not caught on Madeira, but arrive there either fresh or 'fresh-frozen'. In a good seafood restaurant, try out the spicy Portuguese fish, tomato, potato and onion stew known as *Caldeirada de Peixe*. It's not cheap, because it contains many different kinds of fish.

Side dishes typical of the island are sweet potatoes (boiled in their skins), or *milho frito*, a diced, fried *polenta* flavoured with herbs. If on your travels you happen to pass a stand at the roadside with women baking hot dough, head for it immediately. The bread is known as *bolo de caco*, and its dough contains sweet potato; eaten hot, with a little garlic butter spread on top, it tastes really delicious.

*Market lady in Funchal*

Madeira grows an abundance of fruit, thanks to its fertile volcanic earth and the mild ocean climate. *Cherimoya* 'custard apple', papaya, guavas, mango, citrus fruits, avocados, bananas, passion fruit, cherries and apricots are produced by the island; however, more often than not, customers in restaurants will be served fruit out of a tin. This is mainly due to the fact that a large proportion of the fruit is exported and fresh fruits are consequently fairly expensive, but you will be able to buy good fresh fruit from the *mercado* in Funchal.

*Prickly pear*

With their meal the Madeirans drink wine (*vinho*) and water (*agua*). Fizzy mineral water is called *agua con gaz*. The island's dry red wine is served by the glass and can only be found in simple rural establishments; more expensive restaurants have wine lists only featuring wines from the Portuguese mainland. One good Portuguese wine is *vinho verde*, a young, slightly fizzy wine with a low alcohol content. White wine (*vinho branco*) and red wine (*vinho tinto*) are usually dry, and most of them are good. Those preferring a sweeter wine should opt for rosé (*vinho rosado*). Madeira's attempts to produce a high-quality table wine of its own are still in their infancy.

Beer (*cerveja*) hardly ever accompanies meals, but is frequently drunk between them. Alcohol-free beers are enjoying great success at present because the number of stop checks on Madeira for drink-driving has recently increased. Spirits, including all the famous international brands, can be found in amazing variety even in the smallest bar. One local speciality is *Aguardente de Cana* (a special Madeiran rum made from sugar cane), which is usually drunk as a *poncha* (mixed with freshly squeezed lemon juice and honey).

After a meal Madeirans often drink coffee; this resembles Italian *espresso* and is known as *Bica*. Those who prefer milk in their coffee should ask for a *Chinesa*.

## The cutlass fish

Madeira's *espada*, or black cutlass fish, has quite an aura of mystery surrounding it. It is caught hardly anywhere else in the world apart from here, and is the speciality of the fishermen from Câmara de Lobos. They leave the coast at night in their small open boats known as *espadeiros* and lower their seemingly endless lines from buoys situated several kilometres offshore. An average line can be around 2km (1¼ miles) long and the lower section of it has lots of short lines equipped with hooks. Squid is used as bait.

*Espadas have sharp teeth*

81

It is said that the *espada* lives up to 2,000m (6,500ft) below the ocean surface. Be that as it may, the fish comes up to a depth of around 600m (2,000ft) at night and, with a bit of luck, two fishermen and one line can catch up to 100 of them in a single night. It's an arduous task, because pulling in the line is usually done by hand and can take several hours.

This black, eel-like fish with its rolling eyes, sharp, rapier-type teeth and delicious white flesh, was discovered by accident during the last century when a fishermen threw out a particularly long line. The *espada* soon developed into the most popular seafood speciality on Madeira, but little was known of its living habits until comparatively recently. On the shelves at the fishmongers it is shiny and black, and scientists have recently been astounded to discover that the *espada* actually glitters very colourfully indeed in its natural environment. When it gets pulled up so quickly on a line it cannot survive the difference in pressure, and suddenly changes colour. Nevertheless, despite the contemporary problem of overfishing, the black cutlass fish seems to be extremely plentiful. Fishermen on Madeira pull in 1,500 tons of it each year.

*Madeira wine*

## Madeira wine

This famous fortified wine – 'Have some Madeira, m'dear' – is never drunk with the meal, but served either as an aperitif or a dessert wine. The fact that it is fortified with brandy during fermentation – once a practical consideration to help preserve it – means that its alcohol content can be as high as 17 percent, and sometimes even more. It is similar to sherry or port, and there are four basic types ranging from sweet to dry. These corresponded originally to the four noble grapes *Malvasia* (sweet, also known as Malmsey), *Boal* (medium sweet, which also comes in a pale version known as Rainwater), *Verdelho* (medium dry, russet-coloured) and *Sercial* (dry and full-bodied). Malmsey wine, in particular, has enjoyed a long period of popularity: as early as 1478, the Duke of Clarence, brother of King Edward IV, chose to be 'drowned in a butt of Malmsey' in preference to being beheaded.

Madeira's fortified wines derive their unique character from the volcanic soil of the island's vineyards and from a unique process of ageing in *estufas* (baking rooms with glass roofs to let in the sun) for several months to as long as 20 years after fermentation. Pure sunlight is decisive in helping the maturing process and every drop of this first-class wine tells how perfectly it has soaked up the sun's rays.

*Boat restaurant, Funchal*

## Restaurant selection

These suggestions for restaurants on Madeira are listed according to the following price categories: $$$ = expensive; $$ = moderate; $ = cheap.

*An Old Town institution*

*Funchal*

**City centre: $O Presidente**, Rua das Mercês 18, tel: 34535. Very popular; **$Bio-Logos**, Rua Nova de São Pedro 34, tel: 36868. Health food.

**Harbour: $$Estrela do Mar**, Largo do Corpo Santo 1, tel: 228255. Seafood; **$$Caravela**, Avenida do Mar 15, tel: 228464. Seafood.

**Hotel zone: $$Summertime**, Estrada Monumental 318, tel: 762476. Very nice terrace; **$$Tropical**, Estrada Monumental 306, tel: 763642. Well known eatery; **$$As Gavinas**, Praia do Gorgulho, tel: 762057. Seafood.

**Avenida do Infante area: $$$Casa Velha**, Rua Imperatriz D Amelia, tel: 225749; **$$$Villa Cliff**, Estrada Monumental, tel: 763025; **$$Salsa Latina**, Rua Imperatriz D Amelia 101, tel: 225182. Provides live Brazilian music on some nights.

*Machico*

**$$$ El Padriño**, Serra Agua. Good seafood; **$$O Xadrez**, Caramachao, tel: 965889. Regional specialities.

# Active Holidays

Whether on land or in water, there are plenty of opportunities for sport on Madeira

## Hiking

Madeira is perfect for a hiking holiday. Its *levada* paths (*see page 9*), laid out next to the narrow irrigation channels, are easy going and hardly slope at all; there are also the old connecting routes between the villages, dizzying coastal paths and the network of lonely but spectacular mountain tracks used by the goatherds.

Many of the walking routes lead through *levada* tunnels, where a torch and waterproof footwear are necessary. A head for heights and sure footing are absolutely essential for the more difficult paths. A variety of hiking guides is available in Madeira's bookshops. Transport possibilities include buses, rental cars or taxis. Some travel agencies in Funchal organise guided hiking tours in the mountains (for more details contact the tourist information office *Turismo*).

*Following the levada trail*

## Swimming

Apart from the tiny Prainha on the São Lourenço peninsula (*see page 48*), Madeira has no sandy beaches at all. Locals and tourists meet up at the rock pools situated in nearly every coastal town. Artificial slopes have been created along the steep coasts, most of them cleverly integrated into the natural rocky landscape, for sea-bathing. The natural sea water swimming pools at Port Moniz, located on the northwest tip of Madeira, are especially beautiful and, it's said, beneficial for your health. For those who prefer sandy beaches, Porto Santo is ideal: it has 8km (5 miles) of golden-yellow sandy beach (*see page 69*).

*Swimming off the rocks*

### Scuba diving

Madeira is popular with divers and recently several measures have been taken to protect aquatic life. There are diving centres at Funchal and Caniço de Baixa, and also on Porto Santo, offering courses, equipment hire and guided diving trips.

### Deep-sea fishing

Day trips can be made from Funchal, Machico and Porto Santo and booked through travel agencies or at Funchal marina. Two of the major operators are Turipesca and Costa do Sol Turismo. Catches include swordfish, tuna and various types of shark. It is also possible to arrange for other, less-involved excursions and special requests are considered.

### Sailing

*Traditional vessels*

Dinghies can be hired from Aquasports in the Lido swimming pool in Funchal during the summer. Trips on old and restored sailing ships, the *Albatroz* and *Mont Carmel*, are also on offer in Funchal marina. Enquire directly on board or at any of the local agencies around the marina. Those arriving with their own boats will find pleasant protected harbours at Funchal and Porto Santo. Madeira has no yacht chartering facilities as yet.

### Windsurfing

The only winsurfing school is located on Porto Santo (Alugabarc on the beach). Visitors can rent surfboards from just about all good hotels, including Hotel Porto Santo, Reid's, the Casino Park Hotel, the Carleton and the Savoy.

### Riding

The Club Ipismo riding club is near Terreiro da Luta. Guests staying at the Dorissol Hotel chain can apply for rides in the Hotel Estrelicia (tel: 765131). Horses can also be hired on Porto Santo, from the Quinta dos Profetas in Ponta (tel: 983165).

### Golf

There are two golf courses: the Palheiro 18-hole course (tel: 792116) east of Funchal and the Santo da Serra course (tel: 552321), which is being extended from 18 to 27 holes. Both are open to guests for a fee; equipment can be hired and lessons to improve your strokes are also available.

### Tennis

Tennis is akin to a national sport on Madeira. Courts are numerous and all the larger hotels have their own. The setting in Quinta Magnólia is quite lovely and the court fees are especially reasonable.

## Nightlife

*Casino de Madeira*

Funchal is the best place for nightlife, most of which is limited to the large hotels and a few clubs in the Old Town. All the big hotels in the city have their own bars or night-clubs offering live music, dancing and many other kinds of entertainment including beauty contests, party games, performances by jugglers and magicians, etc. The **Casino Park** and **Savoy** hotels both have famous nightclubs. Good discotheques can be found in the **Madeira Carlton** and the **Madeira Palacio** hotels.

Young people tend to go to the discotheque in the **Duas Torras Hotel**, on Estrada Monumental, **Art Rock**, on Caminho Velho da Ajuda, or to the **Formula 1**, Ruo do Favilha 5. Bingo, roulette and blackjack can be played at the **Casino da Madeira** (daily 8pm–3am, minimum age 18, passport required); **Baccara**, the nightclub next door to the casino, provides laser and dance shows.

Folklore and *fado* can be enjoyed in the hotels as well as in various pubs and cabarets in Funchal and Machico; if you've got your heart set on a night of *fado*, pay a visit to **Marcelino**, Travessa das Torres 22, in Funchal. Right next door you'll find the **Jazz-Club**; with a little luck you will arrive on time for a jam session. Folklore evenings are organised by local travel agencies.

In Machico, there's the **Piccadilly** disco in the Hotel Dom Pedro; the A Viela bar in Agua de Pena provides *fado* and Brazilian music; and the **Avo do Fado**, Sitio da Torre, tel: 962230, also does *fado*.

If you are looking for a place in which to relax and have a drink after dinner, you could go to a pub. Recommended for the young and young-at-heart is **Berilights**, on the cor-ner of Estrada Monumental and Rua do Gorgulho, which offers good music. The homesick British can choose be-tween **Joe's Bar** and the **Pombo Mariola**.

**85**

*Funchal by night*

# Getting There

## By air

The Portuguese national airline, TAP, has a virtual monopoly on scheduled services in and out of Madeira, linking Funchal with Lisbon. It also has flights to London, Paris, Lyon, Madrid, Geneva, Zurich and Frankfurt.

The cheapest and often the quickest flights to Madeira will be charter flights, which take about four hours from Northern Europe. Consult a travel agent or the travel pages of the national newspapers for details. For some reason, cheaper charter flights leave from Brussels.

A taxi to Funchal from Santa Catarina airport costs around 2,500 escudos. The bus is much cheaper and stops right outside the airport but the timetable is incomprehensible, so all you can do is admire the view until a bus comes. Package tourists will have their own transport from the airport arranged for them.

## By sea

Surprisingly, there are no passenger ferries to Madeira, but Funchal harbour is a famous anchorage for cruise ships, including the Queen Elizabeth II. Some of these ships will take passengers who don't want to stay on board for the complete cruise: it is therefore possible to rendezvous with one or other of them at departure ports on mainland Europe and arrive on Madeira in style.

# Getting Around

## By air

Day trips to Porto Santo can be booked through travel agencies on Madeira. The local airline LAR runs several connections a day between Funchal and Porto Santo; the price of a return ticket is around £50. More information can be obtained from TAP, Av das Comunidades Madeirenses 8-10, tel: 230151.

## By sea

There's a hydrofoil connection from Funchal to Porto Santo once a day, and twice a day in summer. The crossing takes 1½ hours. During the summer there are also several excursions by boat along the south coast of Madeira.

## By bus

In Funchal, the orange-coloured buses (*Horarios do Funchal*) travel in great numbers from the city centre to the outlying suburbs. The termini are along the Avenida do Mar next to the harbour. Timetables and maps are available

*Opposite: flower stall in Funchal*

*The national carrier*

87

*Funchal airport*

at the stops. Weekly tickets and discount tickets can be purchased at the green sales pavilions on the Avenida do Mar (remember to bring your passport). Buses heading east leave from the bus station in the Rua Joao Brito Camara; those headed west leave from the bus station in the Rua Dr Manuel Pestana Junior. Buses for Canico, Camacha/Santo da Serra and Faial/Santana leave from the harbour promenade opposite the Old Town.

For more information contact the Funchal tourist office (Avenida Arriaga 18, Monday to Saturday 9am–7pm, Sunday and public holidays 9am–1pm, tel: 225658, fax: 232151).

### By taxi

*Taxis are relatively cheap*

Taxis on Madeira are relatively cheap. Trips within the Funchal area are metered, and the basic charge is Esc 200. Enquire locally about hiring a taxi for longer distances, across or around the island; for such trips it pays to discuss the price in advance.

### Car hire

The best, though by no means the cheapest, way to get to know Madeira is by rented car. Cars can be hired from £25 a day (petrol is extra), and most of them are in good condition. Drivers have to be aged 23 or over, and need to provide their national driving licence. It's worth paying a bit extra for comprehensive insurance.

### Driving tips

Drive carefully and be considerate. It is not unusual to hear someone honk when approaching a sharp curve or have them overtake you in a daredevil manoeuvre. In spite of the distinctly anarchic driving style of many Madeirans, serious accidents are a rare occurrence.

*Shuttle helicopter to Porto Santo*

# Facts for the Visitor

## Travel documents

For stays not exceeding three months, citizens of the European Union only need to bring their passports. A residence permit is needed where longer stays are intended. Visitors from Australia, Canada and the US are given a 60-day tourist visa when they enter the islands.

## Customs

Goods being brought into Madeira are not subject to tariffs as long as they were bought within the European Union. The same applies to objects being taken back to EU countries from Madeira for personal use. Restrictions apply to non-EU citizens and there are also limits on what may be exported duty-free.

*Planning itineraries*

## Tourist information

Tourist information abrioad is provided by the Portuguese Trade and Tourism Office.

**In the UK:** 2nd Floor, 22–25A Sackville Street, London W1X 2LY, tel: 0171 494 1441; fax: 0171 494 1868.
**In the US:** 590 Fifth Avenue, 4th Floor, New York, NY 10036 4704, tel: 212 354 4403; fax: 212 764 6137.

In Madeira, contact the local *Turismo*.
**Funchal:** Avenida Arriaga 16, tel: 225658.
There are branch offices in Câmara de Lobos, Machico, and at Santa Catarina airport.
**Porto Santo:** Delegacão do Governo, tel: 982361.
*Opening times:* 9am–8pm, Sundays and holidays 9am–6pm. Smaller *Turismo* offices are open only on regular working days.

## Currency and exchange

*Most banks close in the afternoon*

The Portuguese unit of currency is the escudo (Esc), which equals 100 centavos. There are 10,000, 5,000, 2,000, 1,000 and 500 escudo banknotes in circulation, and 200, 100, 50, 20, 10, 5, 2, 1 and 50 centavo coins. Banks accept cash, eurocheques (up to a value of Esc 30,000 per cheque) and traveller's cheques; the exchange rate is a bit better where cheques are involved. Bank cards with PIN codes can be used at automatic tellers (*caixas electronicas*) for withdrawing money. Credit cards are also becoming increasingly popular as a means of payment.

Portuguese money may be taken in and out of the country up to a limit of Esc 100,000. There is no limit on the amount of money that may be imported in foreign currency in cheque or cash form. Money up to the value of Esc 500,000 may be taken out. For larger sums, special application has to be made.

*Clock shop*

## Opening times

*Shops* on Madeira are usually open Monday to Friday 9am–1pm and 3–7pm and on Saturday 9am–1pm. Shopping centres are open longer in the evenings and also at the weekends.

*Banks* are open Monday to Friday 8.30am–2.45pm; some stay open until 7pm and are also open on Saturday morning.

*Post office* opening times vary a great deal, but the general rule is Monday to Friday 9am–7pm.

## Public holidays

New Year's Day, 25 January, Shrovetide, Good Friday, 25 April, 1 May, 10 June, Corpus Christi, 1 July (Madeira Day), 15 August, 21 August (Funchal Celebration Day), 5 October, 1 November, 1 December, 8 December, 25 December and numerous local public holidays.

*Shades for the summer*

## Shopping

Lidossol and Cavalinho are the new temples of pilgrimage for many Madeirans at the weekends – both of them are supermarkets, massive by the island's standards, which stay open right into the evening on Saturday and Sunday. They are located next to the public swimming centres in Funchal – swimming and shopping are a popular combination. Until only a few years ago Madeira had tiny little shops that only stocked the necessaries, and fresh food was bought at the market. Times are hard now for retail traders, because they can't keep up with the selection available at the supermarkets. Madeira's small shops are steadily being forced to close. However, there are still plenty of local markets with Funchal's *Mercado dos Lavradores* (Workers' Market) open daily.

*The market is open daily*

Shops for anything slightly out of the ordinary will be found in Funchal. Famous foreign fashion firms have boutiques there, but the prices for brand-name goods tend to be rather higher than those in the UK. Portuguese-made shoes are good value

**Souvenirs:** Madeiran embroidery (*see page 74*) has its price. The leaden seal is its proof of authenticity, and the largest assortment can be found in the sales rooms of the embroidery factories in Funchal. Wicker products (*see page 74*), also hand-made on Madeira, come in an amazing number of shapes and sizes. They can be purchased at Camacha, where they are made, or in Funchal at the market. Bulky goods can be shipped home as ocean freight or sent by air (contact the relevant airline for more information).

Madeira wine can be carried home from the island in special cartons with carrying handles. The best place to buy it is from an export firm's tasting room in Funchal.

Flowers are packed into containers and are easy to transport. Bird of paradise flowers, orchids and flamingo flowers can be obtained in the market hall at Funchal or from the small flower market near the cathedral.

*Strelitzia*

## Tipping
Service is included in the bill at hotels and restaurants, but satisfactory service is usually rewarded with an extra five to ten percent of the final amount. Porters expect around Esc 100 per suitcase and chambermaids around Esc 500 a week.

## Postal services
Post offices can be recognised by the CTT sign outside. They are the only places, apart from licensed sales outlets, where stamps (*selos*) can be obtained. Be certain to write *Via Aerea* on all airmail items.

*Convenient for stamps*

## Telephone
International calls can be made from public phones using 50-escudo coins, but you'll have more success from phone boxes marked 'Credifone', which take phone cards available from all post offices and some stationery shops. You can also make calls – international and local – from the post offices. To call direct to the UK, dial 0044, plus the area code without the zero, then the phone number. For the US and Canada, dial 001 plus the full phone number. AT&T, tel: 05017–1288; MCI, tel: 05017–1234; Sprint, tel: 05017–1877.

**91**

*Remote connections*

## Time
Madeira time is the same as British time, that is one hour behind CET (Central European Time).

## Electricity
Most hotels have 220V AC. Adaptors can be bought at all major airports.

## Clothing
Madeira experiences really sunny summer weather only between July and September. At other times of the year it's advisable to have a pullover and a light jacket at the ready. The weather can get cool up in the mountains during the winter. Rain showers don't usually last long, but come prepared. Formal attire is only required in the luxury hotels.

## Photography
Films and photographic equipment cost a lot more on Madeira than they do in the UK. Some types of battery are also difficult to get hold of.

## Newspapers, radio, and television

English newspapers are available with only a day's delay. Ask at a *Turismo* or hotel for information sheets in English.

Local radio stations broadcast excellent music programmes and a radio service for tourists is in the pipeline. BBC World Service can be received on shortwave.

*Yesterday's news*

The sole regional TV channel produces good English and American films with subtitles, and the top hotels receive satellite TV.

## Crime

Madeira is a lot safer than many other Southern European holiday destinations, but it's best to abide by the common-sense rules all the same: keep money and valuables in the hotel safe.

## Medical assistance

In an emergency, many hotels will arrange for their hotel doctors to come, but this can be expensive. As a rule, doctors must be paid on the spot. Ask for a receipt to give to your health insurance company back home. If possible, before seeing a doctor, go to the DRSP, Centro de Saude de Bom Jesus, Rua da Hortas 67, tel: 29161 (9.30am–noon and 2pm–4pm). Here you can obtain a medical insurance booklet valid everywhere in Portugal.

In an emergency go directly to one of the hospitals or private clinics; there are health centres (*Centro de Saude*) in all the major towns. The regional hospital in Funchal is at Av. Luís de Camoes, tel: 742111.

For minor aches and pains, English is spoken at the Centro Medico da Se, located right next to the cathedral, tel: 982211.

Chemists can be found everywhere on Madeira and on Porto Santo. There is always one which is open round the clock; the current schedule is posted on every chemist's door. There are many medications that should be available only with a prescription but which you can often get without one.

## Emergencies

Police, tel: 115.
Ambulance, tel: 41115.
General emergencies, tel: 20000. A total of 115 hospitals and clinics are linked to this number.

## Diplomatic representation

**United Kingdom:** Avenida de Zarco 2, CP417, Funchal, tel: 221221.
**United States of America:** Avenida Luis Carmes, Edificio Infante B1/B/AP/B/4, Funchal, tel: 743429

## Accommodation

*In the heart of the hotel zone*

Package holidays guarantee cheaper accommodation. Booking individually means paying the full listed hotel price, whereas travel agents hand on part of their discounts to the customer. Those still intending to organise their own accommodation on Madeira are advised to book in good time, because sometimes (Christmas, Easter, summer holidays) the island can be completely booked up. Anyone planning an island round trip with short stays in various places should never arrive in the smaller towns and villages without having booked in advance, because there are few rooms and they tend to vanish quickly. Package tours that include car rental and accommodation in various parts of the island really are a worthwhile alternative.

**93**

*Modern developments*

### Hotels

In Portugal hotels are classified on a scale from one to five stars. Funchal does have a few one- and two-star hotels, but most are three- or four-star. The five-star establishments are very grand indeed, with liveried chauffeurs and doormen, champagne receptions with the hotel manager and a discreet, cosmopolitan atmosphere. Most of the better hotels on Madeira are located in Funchal's hotel zone, but there are several at Caniço and Machico, and on Porto Santo, too. Prices can vary a lot within the individual categories depending on location and room furnishings. Single rooms are of limited availability and are also relatively expensive.

*Reid's: a venerable institution*

### Apartments

Life is a lot more relaxed in an apartment. Many hotels have turned their rooms either partially or completely into self-catering studio apartments and renamed themselves *Aparthotels*. They provide the usual hotel service and are

grouped into categories of one to four stars. There are large apartment complexes in Funchal (Pico dos Barcelos), Machico (Matur) and Caniço (Galosol). Self-catering is a good idea whenever longer stays on the island are involved, or for health reasons; it doesn't save all that much money since restaurant prices on Madeira are still quite reasonable. Buying food in Funchal is no problem at all, but the assortment tends to be rather less varied in other places.

## Boarding houses

Simple boarding houses in Portugal are known as *pensao*, and a *residencial* is a more glorified version. They can have between one and four stars. There are many boarding houses in Funchal and many of the smaller towns on the island; their guests generally tend to be locals. Prices for a double room with bath vary between Esc 4,000 and Esc 10,000.

## Private accommodation

This is extremely hard to find. With luck, an address can sometimes be obtained from cab drivers or tourist information offices, or just by word of mouth. This really is the best way of coming into proper contact with the islanders. Private rooms are comparatively cheap, too (around Esc 3,000 for a double room); accommodation does tend to be a bit basic, however.

## Restored mansions

There has been a trend on Madeira recently towards restoring the island's dignified old mansions – many of which were due for demolition – and converting them into hotels, and the money to do so is now available from the EU. Several of these mansions, predominantly in Funchal and around Caniço, are already open. The rooms don't usually have their own private balconies, but the grounds, full of old trees, are accessible to guests.

## Mountain huts

There is not a lot of accommodation available on Madeira for hikers up in the mountains. Several well-equipped *pousadas* (Portuguese government-run hotels) can be found at Pico do Arieiro and near Serra de Agua (*Vinhaticos*). Timely booking is advisable. Accommodation at the mountain hut on the Pico Ruivo has to be officially applied for in advance at the *Turismo* in Funchal. The government also owns huts in Queimadas, Ribeiro Frio, Rabacal and on the Bica da Cana, and they are usually used by government officials at the weekends. For these it is essential to book well in advance at the Governo Regional, Quinta Vigia, Av. do Infante, Funchal.

## amping

[M]adeira has one camp site at Porto Moniz, and on Porto [S]anto there's a site right next to the beach in Vila Baleira. [A] lot of locals like to camp here during the summer hol[id]ays; during the rest of the year the sites are largely empty. [C]amping up in uninhabited areas of the mountains is tol[er]ated as a rule, but it's not all that easy to find a suitable [pl]ace to pitch camp because of the rough terrain.

## [H]otels in Funchal

*Sea views available*

[M]ost hotels are west of the town centre in the old and [th]e new hotel areas, though there are some (mostly [ch]eaper) ones in the centre too. Here is a brief list of some [of] Funchal's hotels in three categories: $$$ = expensive; [$]$ = moderate; $ = cheap.

*The Casino Park Hotel*

**$$$Reid's Hotel**, Estrada Monumental, tel: 763001, fax: [76]4499. Top traditional hotel on the island; **$$$Casino [P]ark Hotel**, Rua Imperatriz D Amelia, tel: 233111, fax: [23]2076. Elegant, near the centre; **$$$Savoy**, Avenida do [In]fante, tel: 222031, fax: 223103. Many British guests, [m]agnificent subtropical garden; **$$$Quinta Bela Vista**, [C]aminho Avista Navois 4, tel: 764144, fax: 765090. Beau[ti]fully restored mansion above the town.

**$$Vila Ramos**, Azinhaga da Casa Branca 7, tel: 764181, [fa]x: 764156. Reliable hotel, quiet location; **$$Quinta do [S]ol**, Rua Dr Pita 6, tel: 764151, fax: 766287. Reliable [ho]tel in a peaceful location; **$$Carlton Palms**, Rua do [G]orgulho, tel: 766100, fax: 766247. Extravagant new [str]ucture right next to the sea in the grounds of an old [m]ansion; **$$Eden-Mar**, Rua do Gorgulho, tel: 762221, [fa]x: 761966. Aparthotel, all rooms with sea view; **$$Quinta da Penha de Franca**, Rua Penha de Franca [4,] tel: 229080, fax: 229261. Old mansion in quiet gar[de]n, new annexe with sea view.

**$Santa Clara**, Calçada do Pico 16B, tel: 224194, fax: [2]43280. Traditional establishment, near the city but quiet; **$Sirius**, Rua das Hortas 31–37, tel: 226117, fax: 223482. [C]entrally located, roof garden; **$Monte Carlo**, Calçada [d]a Saude 10, tel: 226131, fax: 226134. Dignified hotel [w]ith good view of city centre.

## [H]otels in Machico

**$$Atlantis**, Agua de Pena, tel: 962811, fax: 965859. [L]arge hotel with a variety of sports facilities; **$$Dom Pe[d]ro Baia**, Vila de Machico, tel: 965751, fax: 966889. [E]xcellent view of Machico Bay; **$Machico**, Prazete do 25 [A]bril, tel: 963511. Simple boarding house in a central [lo]cation.

# Index